A Wulfrunian way

'Poetically thinking,
wandering in Wolverhampton'

by

Robbie Kennedy Bennett

Robbie KB

Scottish Wulfrunian
Poetic Writing of Robbie Kennedy Bennett
since 1989

All rights reserved
The moral right of the author has been asserted

Poetic Writing of Robbie Kennedy Bennett

No part of this book may be used or reproduced in any manner without written permission, except in the case of brief quotations with reviews. The unauthorised reproduction or distribution of this copyrighted work is illegal. No part of this book may be scanned, uploaded or distributed via the internet or any other means, electronic or print, without the publisher's permission.

A Wulfrunian Way ©
Robbie Kennedy Bennett 2020

ISBN: 9798584834807

Introduction

This book is a collection of my poetic and story writing based on, and around my hometown of Wolverhampton. As time passed I became more knowledgable of my Wulfrunian roots and ancestors. Where and how they lived makes me want to revisit that time - or imagine it. I have a sporting background (football and running) but in later years my only form of exercise is walking and writing about it afterwards.

It was actually the content of a popular poem of mine, plus the sad start in life for my Mother and the kindness afterwards, that influenced me to produce this publication that links family and Wolverhampton.

People of Wolverhampton are known as Wulfrunians as the town was named after the Anglo-Saxon noblewoman and landowner Lady Wulfrun(a) in 985AD. The place itself was Hēatūn / Heantune (or High Town) becoming Wulfruna's Heantune. You can see from there the name of Wolverhampton developing. A statue of Lady Wulfruna by Sir Charles Thomas Wheeler KCVO CBE PRA stands outside the main entrance of St Peter's Church. The gold and black colours of Wolverhampton Wanderers Football Club originated from the town's motto of 'Out of Darkness Cometh Light.' Wolverhampton was given city status for the new millennium in 2000.

Content of Odes or Story

1 - A Wulfrunian Way
2 - Ladies Wore Dresses and Blokes Were Smart
NEW CROSS TO CODSALL, FOR THE INNOCENT
3 - Holy Trinity Church and Heath Town in a Former Time
4 - Shanks's Pony, Aye if Only
5 - In Search of Sampson Darby and Sarah Wheaton
6 - Rough Hills Days - Parkfield Nights
7 - My Heart and Soul
8 - Many Times
9 - We Knew We Had Love From Our Mom and Dad
10 - I'm Going to Catch a Train
11 - The All Saints Line
12 - A Time For Williams
13 - My Heath Town Hike
14 - Eating My Heart Out in Eastfield
15 - My Christmas Wish of a Story
16 - Andy Stewart Sang on Hogmanay
17 - Sweet Mary, Will You Wait With Me to See Lucy
18 - Praise the Skilled Men of the Georgian Era
19 - I'd Be Fifteen At The Time
20 - I Never Knew Him as Grandad
21 - The Calling of Time by Barb or Fred Lavender
22 - Our Shaz, the Friendliest Angel in Heaven
DELTA
23 – The Tavern To Me Is Still Standing Over There
24 - A Tribute to Nan and Grandad
25 - Sarah Ann and the September Sky
26 - She's Somewhere Near
27 - My Story
TREAT YOURSELF AULD LAD
28 - Joseph Williams, a Blacksmith from Stevens Gate
29 - Owen, Williams an' Darby
30 - Joseph Williams, Sarah Ann Darby, I Hear ...

31 - An Owen Kept Goal for Chillington Tool
32 Owens of All Saints
OWENS MEET IN ST ANDREWS
33 Always at Molineux
34 - A Badge on a Blazer, a Shirt and Tie
35 - Especially Rachael
36 - My Bilston Road Beginning
37 - When Are You Going to Find Time
38 - East Park Happiness
39 - The Grooves in the Old Corner Brick
40 - Poppies by All Saints Church in July
41 - The Wolvo Old Roads
OFTEN AT ALDERSLEY
FAIRIES FIELD
42 - Here's to More Knowing of Mr Owen
43 - The Distance to Town Seemed Longer .....
SOME SORT OF WULFRUNIAN TRAIL
44 - Kiss Jane Corbett, The Beautiful Bride
45 - The Rowley Name
46 - Oneself and the Sense of Morality
47 - Stars Over Calvados
48 - Be Yourself
49 - Beyond the Reflection
50 - Th' Laddie in th' Cardigan
51 -King of Bilston
BUILDINGS AND PAST TIMES
52 - Give Me a Room Back in Time
53 - Definitely Parkfields, Not San Francisco
54 - Staffordshire Looks Me In The Face
55 - As Usual She Had That Lovely Bright Smile
56 - Here's to the Scotsman Who
57 - Out of Nowhere
58 - The All Saints River of Life
59 - Waiting to See Queen Elizabeth
60 - Remembering Wolverhampton
THE POET IN THE PAPER
61 - Hey, Have a Guess What, I Walked to Woodcross
62 - My Recognisable Wolverhampton
63 - The Queue to Blaydon Road Bridge
64 - Wulfruna Street Memories
65 - You Have My Respect Sir
WITH POPSKI'S PRIVATE ARMY

66 - Victory For That Hard Done Generation
67 - One Early Morn Near Inverkeithing
68 - Openly Honest
69 - A Half-Filled Pocket-Money Tin
70 - On This Day of a Previous Century
71 - A Good Reason to Pause, at Caledonia Street
72 - A Violin Plays
73 - At The Very Least There's a Road Sign
74 - The Blue Brick Viaduct at Dunstall
75 – Star of The Village Pete Doody
EDWARD OWEN
76 - Only a Stone's Throw Away is a Church
A TREE PLANTED IN HEAVEN (Ben Owen)
PROUD WULFRUNIAN

A Wulfrunian Way

> 'It's fair to say, that everyday,
> we've lived our life a Wulfrunian way.'

'THE USE OF TRAVELLING is to regulate imagination by reality, and instead of thinking how things may be, to see them as they are.' That is a quote of a famous son of Lichfield, Samuel Johnson 1709-1784. Before noticing his portrait painted by Sir Joshua Reynolds on display in Lichfield Cathedral; we had rested on a bench at Minster Pool. So to 'regulate my imagination by reality,' I was impressed of how it must have looked like in the 14th century and onward, after Bishop Walter Langton's day, and as it is now. We had parked up near by, walked the interesting streets, went in a few shops and refreshed in a cafe. Sun was out making the September temperature comfortable for our four-hour, fully paid-up, car-parking charge visit. There was a service in process in the cathedral so it was a good idea when I thought of switching my mobile phone to 'silent, just in case.' Along with all the interesting architecture etc.; we noticed cushions and searched for Deaneries where we are connected to. I see poet Anna Seward was instrumental in landscaping Minster Pool and take in Samuel Johnson's quote about regulating imagination by reality. All said, I search for a few words of mine. Beyond the pool, the garden of remembrance and mature trees is the only medieval three-spired cathedral in the United Kingdom. This commonplace poet won't ever influence the landscaping and capture the ambiance of anything such as lovely as this; I see the quality of it now, and imagine it in past-time; inspiring me to write.

> "Write you commonplace poet;
> where e'er you travel, write!"

So that's what I do - I write, to remind me of people and places, just as I did above after Lynne and I had that drive out to Lichfield. Mentioning past-time; I wish that Wolverhampton was more like it was in the old photographs and I could walk into them and spend time with my Wulfrunian ancestors; put on our Sunday clothes and stroll about the surrounding parks. Wolverhampton has some historic landmarks – it's easy to see as to why going to town was a special event. When I admire those buildings, I am well aware that family before me have done so too.

A Wulfrunian Way

A Wulfrunian Way

A WULFRUNIAN WAY; A moment from 2016, reading through some writing of mine form a couple of years ago and the mention of my poem 'A Wulfrunian Way' that keeps in mind my Wolverhampton kin;

St Peter's Church chimed midday as I stepped outside of the Art Gallery. After a few weeks of my Scottish ancestral writing which had led to being featured in newspapers in Fife, it was time to turn to my Wulfrunian roots. I hadn't been up Wolverhampton for a few months and was quite looking forward to spending a couple of hours up there. I recalled times when as a teenager meeting school friends in town and looking down from the walls at St Peter's. I was an active lad back then and can remember jumping down onto the grass. Those days are well gone now!

I thought about the old market that was there where the Civic Centre is. My relations would be on buses back and forth to go shopping. Old pictures of Wulfrunian soldiers before they went off to fight in the First World War. I wonder if Benjamin James Owen was there that day? Soon I was to spend a pleasant hour looking around the Art Gallery then catching up with my cousin Cherry Ann from the Owen family who works in the cafe. Just being around the surroundings and hearing the bells of St Peter's chime brought to mind a poem of mine from 2006, also titled 'A Wulfrunian Way.'

(1) **A Wulfrunian Way** ©

I descend from a working class background;
I grew up in a town of my mother's line.
I live everyday a Wulfrunian way,
And there is nothing that I want that is not mine.
There are family names scattered all around,
Roots of mine are in this town,
Within the soil deep in the ground.
Goodyear company my grandad served,
Long service recognition was well deserved
I can always find a family name,
From Bushbury and Graiseley to Steelhouse lane.
Williams, Rowley and Owen have seen,
World wars and coronations of Kings and Queen,
We've walked down St Peter's steps to the market,
Shopped at the open stalls.
Waited at the stops for trolley buses,
And sat on the old church walls.
We've saw vehicles drive down Dudley Street
And been struck by the light in the old Arcade.
Many a relation at All Saints was taught,
And many a present from Beatties was bought.
We've stood on the terraces at Molineux,
The great days my relations have seen.
We were here before the racetrack at Dunstall,
Before greyhounds and speedway at Monmore Green.
The Mander Centre came,
And shoppers descending from a family name.
Williams, Rowley and Owen have been,
The town of Wolverhampton changes we've seen.
Prince Albert on his horse wasn't always there,
He's moved a few times since he came to Queen Square.
New buildings in town that's now called a city,
Some perhaps fine and others not so pretty.

A Wulfrunian Way

Relations have worked at Chubbs,
And been the licensee of pubs and clubs.
The Royal Hospital treated our troubles and woes,
Our cuts and scars and nursed our bloody nose.
It's fair to say, in every way,
We've worked and toiled and earned our pay.
And It's fair to say, that everyday,
We've lived our life a Wulfrunian way.

Albert, Prince Consort,
(by T. Thorneycroft in Queen Square)
Erected by Subscription
Inaugurated by The Queen 1866

My poem 'A WULFRUNIAN WAY' was written in 2006 and I was pleased that it made Carl Chinn's Black Country Memories page in the Express & Star. For those outside the Wolverhampton area, it is our local newspaper founded in 1889. Carl added the picture of the open air market in Wolverhampton in 1910 with St Peter's Church in the background. What strikes me most is the last line underneath the photograph; "Robbie's forebears would have known this scene well." In the article leading up to my poem, Carl has printed something else that is significant. "In writing it he held fast belief that the past is an important part of the present and the future."

This book is a follow on to **Awa' th' Rough Hills an' Awa'** and **On a Wolverhampton Journey**; both having videos on You Tube should you wish to see more of my hometown and places that I write of. Other titles of mine can be found at the rear of this book. With the advertising over with, I shall continue; now where was I? Was it Lichfield? "No" I hear said, "you're in Wolverhampton now, imagining how it used to be, in days of your ancestors." I didn't really hear that, it's this author's way of making the start of this book more interesting. Allow me now to take us back to yesterday afternoon of the first Friday in 2020. The following post of mine was made on social media proving that this book was brewing;

Without knowing; but to be honest I did know in a little way, that I have another book 'on the go'. I don't think of myself as a serious writer but there are pieces of my writing taking place. The last 12 months has been spent on my back operation, recovery and retirement from Wolves. I've got myself organised; I realised that **OUR TRAIL TO SCOTLAND** was more advanced and almost ready so we pushed it over the line! What do I do now? The writer in me has plans; the runner in me says push on and do your best;

the footballer in me says appeal whether it's your way or not! The grandad in me says get the grandkids writing; The writer in me says, you have another book 'on the go' haven't you? Yes I admit; it just happened to be there, and quite well organised. It's WOLVERHAMPTON based and more advanced than I thought. I'm into my 31st year of writing; not the best poet ever and probably nearer the worst, and no one can tell my story, not a word of my story. Every like and comment of my writing I find is inspirational, I trust that you have found something in there for you.

    I received lovely messages from relations on my Bennet side, Joan and Sandy Grabert in Louisiana and others of encouragement. What came first though was from Chris Gayle-Jebbison who I first met in Toronto while I was working for Wolves; *Thank you, for sharing this Bob. You are a writer!!! I pray your recovery has been a speedy one. Much love and blessings!!!*

    I woke early next morning to find that Helen Muir had commented. She is a granddaughter of Len Muir who I worked with at Delta when I was in my early twenties. I wrote about Len and years later I found Helen on social media and introduced myself. She was about to move from Tettenhall to Weymouth and we were both overjoyed at our meeting each other. Many years had passed since I was to write in the bibles' of Helen and her sister Jayne when they were children. Their grandpa taught me so much about life, and I still call on our days together. It just goes to show that places of work can lead to a lifetime of friendship.

    Happy New Year Robbie xxx I often pick up and read your books. My 'step' dad really enjoyed them too. Thank you for taking the time to document your life for us all to share. All too often, memories are lost amongst busy lives. I'm grateful for you taking the time to share such wonderful words in your books xxx

A Wulfrunian Way

(2) Ladies Wore Dresses and Blokes Were Smart ©

How times have changed
so obvious when looking at photographs;
the fondness of those years,
and loved ones who you thought would live forever!
A get-together, those jolly social gatherings,
where cousins meet their extended family;
looking at each individual one by one,
kids grown up, time moved on.
One thing that always touches my heart,
ladies wore dresses and blokes were smart,
like film stars, advertising their own movie.
Oh, to revisit days gone by,
men in a suit with a shirt and tie,
each had style, so obvious to see,
and a loved one's smile...that's aiming at me.

A Wulfrunian Way

Joseph Williams & Sarah Ann Williams (nee Darby)

I suppose it was because of mom's adoption in the family that we appeared to have many cousins. There was the ones from Rowley and our Owen family scattered around the town; also Darby, living nearby on Pond Lane. Mom's Rowley sisters are Shirley and Janet and the family home was on First Avenue, Low Hill. This house was knocked down to build maisonettes which disappointments me so much when driving by as our past is less imaginative. Nan and grandad were re-housed in a maisonette near the Scotlands. Mom's first and second mothers, Sarah Ann (Nancy) and Jane (Gin), were Williams, children of Joseph Williams and Sarah Ann Darby along with Ethel, Nell, and Mill. As children we were close to the family of Aunt Mill and uncle Ern as they lived near us on Thompson Avenue. So we had more cousins by the name of Hodgetts.

Mom's Owen sister was Marion (Marie), she married Doug Beszant, and their brothers were Ben, Ken (Monk), Jim and Eddy, living as I mentioned earlier around the town. Uncle Ben was often at our house, living with us for a time, and he used to take me to Wolves games. I can recall that he also drove me to my football trials at Shrewsbury and Walsall. At Shrewsbury we met an Owen relation who I think was Jim and his son Paul was also on trial that day. Ken lived in Victoria Road, Bradmore; he married Sybil Arnold. Jim lived in Low Hill and quite a character he was; he married Nell Evans. Eddy often called, always happy and smiling; he married Dorothy Clarke.

As you can imagine, it was difficult to decide where to start this book. Should it be with the furthest generation I can find? Such as Jas Scott and Sarah Thursfield in the 1700's, then discover one further, William and Elizabeth Darby, or should I step in and out between past and modern day? It had to be the latter as that is how I was to find our ancestral background and also how I write. Beforehand there is a part extract of mom's writing below;

'Off Eagle Street, All Saints, behind where the Summer House pub is now, was a court yard of small houses, each with a brew house. It was a brick building with a boiler to do the washing. The houses had two upstairs and two downstairs rooms, the back one in the yard, the front in Steelhouse Lane. I was born in the end house number 2 or 22? Court, Eagle Street. It was larger than the other houses as it used to be a pub. Ken was a builder and said that when it was demolished a bag of sovereigns was found in the chimney.

The house was divided into separate dwellings; my family lived there, also aunt Ethel's. My mother (Sarah Ann) died there in 1929 when I was 6 weeks old. Grandmother Williams (Sarah Ann Darby) also died there in 1931, although she lived at 144 Steelhouse Lane on the corner of Major Street. All of these houses have long gone. My father (Benjamin James Owen) was left with six children, Ben the eldest was 11, Jim, Ken, Eddy, Marie and myself- Dorothy. My Aunt Jane (Gin) and Uncle George took me to live with them, they had only been married two weeks, they adopted me when I was three, became my mom and dad, gave me a loving and happy home, a few years later they had two children, Shirley and Janet. Grandad Williams (Joseph) also lived with us.

My real father married again to Maud Allen, sister of Uncle Sid, husband of Aunt Ethel. They had two children, Sidney and Michael. My mother was 33 when she died of pneumonia, my father was 40 when he died, also of pneumonia. He was wounded very badly in the First World War and only had one lung. I was six when he died, I have a faint recollection of him. I think that Marie took me once to meet Aunt Maud and to be fair, she had taken a lot on, she had one daughter herself and my father's five.'

Mom (Dorothy) with Jane/Gin.

Marion, Shirl and Mom (Dorothy)
in Foster Road

NEW CROSS TO CODSALL, FOR THE INNOCENT;

At Jordans Bridge (classed as a Grade II Listed Building), I arrived at the same time as a barge about to enter the No 8 lock. We politely spoke to each other as we passed by. Suddenly there was a sound of surging water which made me turn around and watch the process of the narrow boat manoeuvring. The bridge brought back an instant memory; suddenly I was a lad again and about to get off the canal where I had cycled from Dixon Street near my childhood home. My Aunt Shirl and Uncle Bill lived in Crown Street and they were about to have a surprise visitor: If only?

Back to the modern day; I was on a 'do something different' type of morning; after needing to get home from New Cross Hospital. I could've drove there and paid the parking charge but decided to use it as a reason to exercise. I got a lift there from Lynne and leisurely made my way inside, taking in the morning sunshine knowing that I was early.

It is May 2017 and the events of the Manchester Arena bombing is playing heavily on my mind; for some, life goes on but sadness fills my heart for those whose family were caught in this wicked act. When first hearing the news I thought of my children and grandchildren as I imagine many of us did. Just as the weather picks up and brightens the world this atrocity darkens it.

I needed a fresh walk, change of view, think outside of my everyday life, step outside of my daily routine; so to walk from the hospital to Wolverhampton Railway Station would be suffice. That proved not to be as I was there quicker that expected and carried on to Bilbrook.

The old road from town to Wednesfield is a route that I used to take occasionally when working at Yale Material Handling. This would be the days before the Black Country Route. I imagined myself as a motorcyclist in the 1980's riding this way to 'clock on' before 8.12am start time.

I looked over at Heath Town Park where I have played and watched a few games of football. I see the church beyond and have searched that graveyard, yet to find an ancestor, eventually doing so. I look over at what used to be The Shoemaker where I had a drink with my 'funny old mate' Len Muir in the 1970's. I approach the lights and see Gareth and myself cycling in the 1960's towards Heath Town Baths; and so it went on all the way to town. It was here that I changed my mind and crossed over to walk alongside the canal; it proved to be a great decision.

Suddenly I was in another world of wildlife and distant traffic sound. I was transported back into another time as I made my way to town. Soon I was beyond the industrial side and into Pendeford. I got off at Bilbrook and was back in my home in Codsall in just over 3 hours. I did stop a couple of times to write and then bumped into an old footballing colleague who was out cycling. All in all it was good to be off the beaten track as they say. I once wrote about 'walking for children to safely play and to live life peacefully.' it still applies. 'I dedicate this walk today, from New Cross to Codsall, to the innocent in Manchester.'

HOLY TRINITY CHURCH AND HEATH TOWN IN A FORMER TIME;

It's Burns Night 2018 tonight and the haggis is yet to be cooked, but before then, my morning was spent in Heath Town just browsing around the church ground and the park. Apparently we have some ancestors here but as of yet not found; the search continues. There was a slight chill in the wind but I had prepared myself well with five layers of clothing. Sunshine accompanied me throughout my time here. I couldn't help but wonder what the surrounding area of the church was like when built between 1850-1852? Looking through the gate and over the Bushbury Road at the war memorial would have been different when first erected as there is now a constant stream of traffic. Those brave soldiers named would have seen it as it was in the old days. I don't profess to be an expert on flowers but there may be snowdrops growing in the church grounds making me look forward to Spring.

(3) Holy Trinity Church and Heath Town in a Former Time ©

Springing up are snowdrops while I'm winding down
easing the January frown around Heath Town
must've been so different a century and half ago
traffic was less, life was slow, imagine it so,
it's easy to see with the eyes and mind of mine
Holy Trinity Church and Heath Town in a former time.

A Wulfrunian Way

(4) Shanks's Pony, Aye if Only ©

Not far from town
in the day when it was
a cart ride, a wee touch
of countryside, not far from
becoming industrial canal side;
in the day when it was
most likely to be Shanks's pony;
if only I could re-visit past time
all I ever think about
most times is past time.
Not far from town
with its own identity,
before we was Wolverhampton city,
in the nitty-gritty of traffic load
on the over populated roads;
more likely to see wild life
aye, hear the singing of birds,
but ark now as I heard,
for a few seconds
all hush, to past time I was lured,
by the song of a thrush
I guess it was that type of bird.
Not far from town
congregations, Victorian dress,
before and after
tears and laughter,
the impressive Lych Gates
all relates to what I seek;
if only they could speak
week upon week, year on year
two by two, one by one,
going back to the day,
when less of the automobile

and it was most likely
to be Shanks's pony;
if only I could re-visit past time
all I ever think about
most times is past time;
if only, aye my friend if only.

IN SEARCH OF SAMPSON DARBY AND SARAH WHEATON;

It was that month that I had sent an email to the church with some names and plot and grave numbers. I had spent some time one morning at Holy Trinity as I had found other family members; I searched without success. It was lovely to be there and a post on Facebook page Wolverhampton Past and Present of my write up and photographs brought a few likes and comments. I received a nice reply next day from Liz Cope and although there are no headstones, the names I had given had been located. On Saturday 3rd February 2018 an appointment was made to meet Liz. A few minutes later she showed me the final resting places of my gg & ggg grandparents. I looked over at the disused Heath Town Baths and Library that had been closed for 15 years. This was where my brother Gareth and I cycled to, to go swimming. It was also the baths that I used as a pupil at Eastfield Secondary Modern School. In all that time it was not known that our ancestors were there; and the many times I have drove by or played football on the park over the road. At the very least they have been located.

A Wulfrunian Way

In Search of Sampson Darby and Sarah Wheaton ©

Robbie Kennedy Bennett

(5) **In Search of Sampson Darby and Sarah Wheaton** ©

Friendliness, helpfulness
in the home and grounds of godliness,
in search of Sampson Darby
not wanting to be beaten
in search of Sampson Darby and Sarah Wheaton.
When the day came, so did the February rain,
worth getting wet for? Of course
and would do so again, full force.
Many helping hands, cutting of trees,
clearing and tidying, preparing for spring
but before then another winter freeze.
Tracing back the ancestors
and where so be their final rest
can prove to be so difficult, a tough old test;
in search of Sampson Darby
not wanting to be beaten
in search of Sampson Darby and Sarah Wheaton.
Hopefulness, devotedness in all you're doing
pursuing all roads and avenues
leaving no stone unturned, when you've found someone
most certainly that find is earned
to stand above them, before them, beside them,
then comes the emotion, to connect with them;
in search of Sampson Darby
not wanting to be beaten
in search of Sampson Darby and Sarah Wheaton.
Sampson, Wolverhampton born,
seems likely you travelled as you got older
on census's both here and in Lancashire

such as 1901 lodging as a moulder;
Sarah, again Wolverhampton born,
a general servant you became,
1872, Church of St Leonard, Bilston in marriage
to Darby you changed your name
when you wed your Sampson;
family were not only Wolverhampton
but in Cheshire, Lancashire and Yorkshire,
that I found, here's a great, great grandson of yours
in February rain on Holy Trinity ground,
with assistance and guidance
Sarah, I've also found your parents
no doubt you were here on that sad date
at the burial of your mother in 1878.
Friendliness, helpfulness
in the home and grounds of godliness,
in search of Sampson Darby
not wanting to be beaten
in search of Sampson Darby and Sarah Wheaton,
yes it was a test, as for now my mind can rest.
Having stood above them,
before them, beside them,
comes once more the emotion, to connect with them.

ROUGH HILLS DAYS – PARKFIELD NIGHTS; This one day I just happened to be driving through Parkfields in Wolverhampton, which was the old area of mine. Boundaries of how far that I could go to became further and further. I don't know if my parents actually gave me any really or it is my imaginative mind. Back to this journey that I am making; waiting for the traffic lights to turn green. I'm a sixty-something man at this time and the teenage pedestrian crossing Parkfields Road that I can see vividly is me! The present day stopped as I was transported back to the late 1960's and early 70's. I had most probably called in at my Aunt Mill and and Uncle Ern's who lived on Thompson Avenue. I sometimes did on route to see my girlfriend.

Aunt Mill and and Uncle Ern's name is Hodgetts and son's Phil and Eric had grown and moved out of the family home. Wendy, Shaz and Mandy were still there and most probably getting ready to go out themselves. Uncle Ern may have encouraged me to come down the garden to see how his plants are growing. Aunt Mill would be reminding me of my younger days when mom called by with me as a toddler. Aunt Mill is on the Williams family line that we have and sister to both my mom's adopted (Jane/Gin) and birth mother (Sarah Ann); parents being Joseph Williams and Sarah Ann Darby.

Traffic lights changed from red to green in a wake-up, time-reminding manner of where I am now in life. The young man who was in front walked on with his day and this sixty - something drove on with mine.

(6) **Rough Hills Days - Parkfield Nights** ©

Traffic light turned to amber then to red
so I stopped instead of going ahead,
from Fighting Cocks and down the Parkfield Road,
all's a little bit different
as the map of life was about to appear and unfold.
For a second or two
former years break through
I knew the area well
another second or two
the years they flew
spinning they were from a film cylinder reel
and sadly an outsider I did feel.
"You're just being melancholy
as you often are"
and there comes me on my way

A Wulfrunian Way

crossing the road in front of my car.
The distance I am walking, that I know
along the Birmingham New Road there I go
imagination, or quite simply do I pretend?
a teenager once again
and off to meet my girlfriend.
"You're just being sentimental
Robbie, that's your style,
keep your eyes on the traffic lights
they'll be changing in a short while"
Aye, but I'm by Thompson Avenue
I would've called in and saw my Aunt Mill,
my Uncle Ern, I wish he was knocking around here still,
I saw him in the Red Lion sometimes,
hark at me, revisiting old times,
why do they surface in my new rhymes?
inner feelings somehow send
a teenager once again
and off to meet my girlfriend.
Amber then to green
a short sort of nostalgic journey I have been,
loved ones came and have sadly gone
in the time of waiting and driving on.
Rough Hills days Parkfield nights
crossed they did in the changing of traffic lights
time, quite simply, I wish that I could lend
a teenager once again
and off to meet my girlfriend.
Lights changed and so have I
the articulated memory lorry had drove on by,
left to right in front of me,
onto the Birmingham New Road,
nothing broken, nowt to mend,
I wish I was a teenager once again
and off to meet my girlfriend.

(7) **My Heart and Soul** ©

My heart and soul is my mom
She gives me the will to always carry on,
My mom to me is my strength
Troubles I learn should be kept at arms length.
My mom to me is all that she should be,
She has wisdom she is wise,
Encourages truth and not lies.
My mom to me is all that she should be,
My heart and soul is my mom
She gives me the will to always carry on,
My mom to me is the confidant I need
For the life that I live and I lead.
My heart and soul is my mom,
She gives me the will to always carry on.

Sarah Ann Williams nee Darby with daughters Sarah Ann (Nancy) & Ethel standing and Jane (Gin) seated.

(8) Many Times ©

Many times I've watched my mother smile,
Many times, many times.
Many times I've watched my mother laugh,
At herself, many times.
A caring and amusing personality,
Oh well, it doesn't matter,
What will be will be.
Many times I watched my mother smile,
Many times.
Many times I've needed her wisdom,
Many times I've needed her presence for a while.
And many times
I've needed her laughter,
And many times I've needed her smile.

(9) We Knew We Had Love From Our Mom and Dad ©

Above everything that we had
We knew we had love from our mom and dad.
Everything that we got
Things we should do and things we should not.
The time to come in
To where have you been?
You're going to school
Or you'll be a fool.
Have you had your wash?
We was still clean
Though we wasn't posh.
We always went to the sea
My mom and my dad, my brothers and me.

We stayed in digs by the docks,
We'd go to the beach
And play on the rocks.
We didn't have loads of dosh
I've told you before we wasn't posh.
We all knew we were glad,
Of the holiday pay our mom and dad had.
'Cause we always went to the sea.
My mom and my dad, my brothers and me.
And above everything that we had
We knew we had love from our mom and dad.

I'M GOING TO CATCH A TRAIN; There's a day approaching when I shall put on my boots and rucksack as I often do in Scotland but this time get on a train from Codsall. I shall arrive soon afterwards in Wolverhampton and make my way through the changeable area to the Royal Hospital building. My mother once called it "my hospital" as I was an active young lad of Rough Hills and often had to visit there. There will be numerous alterations to the old roads but for me it will be the terraced time of the 1950's & 60's, even earlier if you count my ancestry. Dressed in a way that last saw me in Galway, Ireland and before then in the east coast Scottish town of Arbroath, I shall take in All Saints Church and schools that prepared me for my lifetime. I wish to find old feelings and imagine old times. Without further ado I shall hand over to my poem and trust that you travel with me and my ideas on that journey;

(10) **I'm Going to Catch a Train** ©

I found in life that there are things in life
that you may not ever find in your lifetime,
unless there's a stroke of luck
paragraph after paragraph for you in a book
that you may overlook if you

A Wulfrunian Way

don't relive your life in your lifetime.
So what are you going to do about it lad
what are you going to do?
your sporting days are o'er
you're fast approaching sixty four,
what are you going to do about it lad,
aye what are you going to do?
I'm going to step out of my Codsall home
and go and catch a train,
I'm going to go to Wolverhampton
sunshine, snow or rain.
I have no friends in high places
but I've had good mates,
family and remember friendly faces,
yes I'm going to catch a train
and ride with a life full of satisfaction and pride
from the Staffordshire countryside,
catching a train,
I'm going to go to Wolverhampton
to relive my life again.
So what are you doing that for
what are your reasons please tell?
here's your chance to shout it out lad
go on now, ring your bell.
I'm going to step off that train
after going to Wolverhampton again,
in my artistic mind my picture paints
to a terraced time of All Saints.
There I shall set myself free
just you watch and see,
the church and schools of a former time
hold family history of mine.
So where are you going to next
I suppose it's to the days before an easy text,
it has all changed about there too

A Wulfrunian Way

then what shall you do?
I'm going to stride down Eagle Street
with the Owen and Williams in mind,
back to previous historic time
'tis easy there to find,
even though old buildings have gone
into bygone days I shall carry on.
So what's new?
that's your writing style,
years and years of memories
you overload your file;
where to then my nostalgic old sir
to anywhere in particular?
Righty-oh, you ask where next I shall go?
towards old Monmore Green,
walking past my old workplace
is strange, a sad and sentimental scene,
for there I was a young man
who comes a stepping towards me this way
if I could do the impossible
I wonder what I would say?
Tell him he's going to marry
and children he'll have as well,
tell him he'll be a devoted family man
I dare you, go on and tell.
No, I shall let him pass me by
with a youthful look in his eye,
if I was to burden him with this knowledge
he'll think I'm a daft old man that's why.
Okay I can see your point
so do you think you are being directed,
have you an important appointment
or are you at a certain time expected?
No, to the East Park where nobody waits
I shall walk through the old iron gates,

A Wulfrunian Way

and hope that I am feeling the joy
of being an active young boy,
I shan't head for the pool or the park
on the band stand this laddie shan't lark,
I shall walk the perimeter you see
circling many memories,
nobody will care if it's me.
Oh yes they will because I will, as I am yourself
not something you can ever discard
collecting dust there upon a shelf,
I am your conscience and ideas too
quite simply old lad, I am you.
In your rucksack and boots
you shall think of your life and roots,
to the Willenhall Road you shall head
family history and life will hover
you shall feel fortunate of being well-fed.
Along Horsley Fields you will feel satisfied
of knowing or not your family that died,
life is not a game that's got to be won
for you old Scottish Wulfrunian son.
Yes you'll be going to Wolverhampton again
once more to jump on a train,
back into your home you shall go
and recall this day as you know.
As you found in life that there are things in life
that you may not ever have found in your lifetime,
you had a stroke of luck
paragraph after paragraph of yours in a book
you didn't forget or overlook
reliving your life, re-visiting your life
in your own way, a noteworthy own way,
in our lifetime.

THE ALL SAINTS LINE; People interest me, especially my ancestors; I'm studying my Wolverhampton family tree that over the years has grown with research. I see road names in an area that's changed plenty in my three score years and more. More so than I could imagine when first I entered those school gates of All Saints, like many in the family before me. I was to play football for the school, and again, so had others before me.

The shops, pubs and houses along Steelhouse Lane that seemed longer when I was a boy. It run like a river with streams of streets that run down to her. The factories that employed so many family members, mine included. Street names call out to me, all because people interest me, especially my ancestors, who were looking through a window; as I look through a window, a colourful window, that they could've been looking at?

I once read that you are never alone when you are reading a book; but how about if it is about your ancestors? This takes you to another level, especially like I have experienced when you are writing it! You learn as you go along; you suddenly realise things that may have been obvious or not. With the names of Owen and Williams, I have been expecting to find a link to Wales, but as of yet I haven't.

The Benjamin Owen who married Sarah Whitehouse was born in 1801 in Hanley Green, in the Potteries, Staffordshire. I believe that it is now known just as Hanley - a constituent town of Stoke-on-Trent. Sarah was born in Bilston in 1804, so was Benjamin, (coal miner), working up there or perhaps down here? Either way, mining had been in the Hanley – Shelton area for centuries before Benjamin Owen was born. The question is, was his father also a miner, in the substantial industrial enterprise of that time? Strange how the mind works, as I wish that I had known this in 1984 when I completed the Potteries Marathon. With our Williams line, births and baptisms appear to be in Wolverhampton and Bilston. I can go back a further generation than the Owens' when John Williams of Ettingshall married Mary Phillips in St Peters.

Although my Darby line is from my great grandmother Sarah Ann Darby, born in Rotherham, it appears to be Wolverhampton except her grandfather Benjamin Derby born in West Bromwich in 1822. His father John Darby born 1782 lived in Horsley Fields. His wife was named Catherine and his parents William and Elizabeth Darby.

The All Saints Line ®

Poetic Writing of Robbie Kennedy Bennett

(11) **The All Saints Line** ©

Relation after relation followed the All Saints line
must've been near on a century of time
relation after relation receiving our education
set was the date, to enter the gate
and go down the All Saints line.
War declared on England in 1914
interestingly this record of the school I have seen
teachers took their part
that August when the term did start
Territorial duty orders came to Mr Piper and Mr Pugh,
sirs, my respect to both of you.
We lived about the area and some married in the church
employed at Edge Tool, after All Saints School.
A grandad of mine was badly injured out in France
presumed dead when found, he had a second chance.
The world at war then a second one
the children came as education carried on
set was the date, to enter the gate
and go down the All Saints line.
We went down the All Saints line, yes indeed
I sometimes return whenever I feel the need
because memories in my opinion is what life is all about
a bell rings, and a hundred children run out,
....no they don't, as it's a writers imagination
seeing me and my relation after relation.
Saying that, it's good to be where schooling all began
on the first playground I had fun and where I ran,
the very wall where I did rest
outside the classroom of my first test,
large rooms with high ceilings
nostalgic feelings are common now
and it all comes back somehow

A Wulfrunian Way

definitely a pleasure of mine
to go back down the All Saints line.
The Right Honourable Lord Barnard
the memorial stone that he laid,
on the 2nd May 1894
made me feel more at home than ever before
when reading the words this time
returning on the All Saints line.
The school may have closed
with the name of All Saints now gone
but Mr Lancaster, education carried on
when you set the date, for me to enter the gate,
I may have peaked too late,
plus, not sure if I was ever capable to do my best
I probably didn't do myself justice
and no doubt failed the test, but thanks for the time
on the All Saints line.

Nellie Broadfield nee Williams, centre of the back row
with her sister Jane (Gin) Rowley nee Williams 3rd from right,
front row, at John Perks Edge Tool, Bilston Rd.

Four sisters nee Williams
From L/R Ethel, ?, Nell, Mill and Gin

(12) **A Time For Williams** ©

The journey of life can be wonderful
and circumstances undesired for at the same time.
'Time,' there's a word that sneaks up on you
and runs away, not a 'thief in the night' type
but surely a 'trickster' of some kind
that steals from you, but also shows you
what it has taken from you.
You turn your back, eat, sleep, go to work
as time moves you forward.
Accepted that new members enter the family
and rightly so, they need love, care and guidance
then off they go on the shared journey of time.
I'd like to be a controller of time
and be capable visiting any which way
in time that I choose, for those that we lose,
brings on that wonderful, painful experience.
Make the old photographs real;
hear the laughter of the old times without the sadness
of losing that chapter of life:
because you feel it, if only for a moment.
I look down the Williams family line that I have;
in a room of Williams family descendants that I have,
all the time thinking of time; this time, Williams time;
desired for I can say but, not in this way.
Assistance, Joseph Williams and Sarah Ann Darby,
your marriage at All Saints in 1893,
your children born afterwards and theirs,
come join us and share this afternoon sunshine.
Samuel Williams, Joseph and John,
three generations further on,
come join us too, bring everyone with you;
share this afternoon sunshine.
Let's see the likeness and compare the clothes of the day,

A Wulfrunian Way

laugh and take away that time in between us;
that time that has seen laughter and tears
yes, and why not, in all of those years?
Samuel of School Road in Tettenhall,
your father John, baptised at Swan Bank
and his father too, Mr John Williams of Ettingshall,
"I'm so pleased to meet you."
"Six generations sir, between you and me,
Wolverhampton has changed a lot, as you can see."
If I was that controller of time
I'd ask of the 17th & 18th century,
Mr John Williams of Ettingshall,
all he could tell, and of Wales,
have we a line sir, in former time?
He may not know of any such link
and that the outskirts of Wolverhampton
are all he and our Williams forefathers have known;
I should imagine he'd be interested to hear
of how his family has grown.
Mr John Williams, born the Georgian era
married at St Peter's in 1812;
please come forward six generations,
sons, daughters, siblings and-so-forth;
further on from his journey of life;
with his lovely wife Mary they
shall add to the ambiance of the occasion;
yes, energetic thoughts they are today.
Mr John Williams of Ettingshall,
at this gathering, a particular undesired time,
he warms in mind, as does the Williams line
in this afternoon sunshine.

John W[illia]ms
[of] Ettingshall

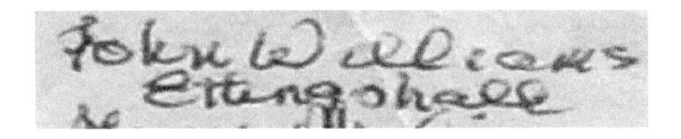

The photograph is of my mother's handwriting when adding John Williams to the family tree. The poem itself (A Time For Williams) came to mind after the funeral of 'our Pat,' as fondly called by my mother; both of Williams descent, with Pat being Nell's daughter. (WILLIS Patricia Ellen nee Broadfield).
Comments; So lovely Rob .. thank you (Vicky). Wonderful words Robbie xxx (Liane). Lovely words Robbie (Deb). Beautiful Rob x (Mandy)

Twelve months to the day of Pat's passing in 2018 we were 'celebrating the life' of her brother Leslie Howard Broadfield 1925 – 2019. Our Les, also brother to Tony who unfortunately died as a child, during the war was in the RAF and remained in the aircraft industry throughout his working life. He was also a talented artist and my timeline on Facebook displays two paintings by Les. One of St Peter's Church and gardens in Wolverhampton and another of the Lomond Hills in Fife. Nieces Vicky (daughter of Pat) and Wendy (daughter of Millicent) were close to Les and his wife Vera.

In March 2019 on the **'Wolverhampton's War – Lost voices from two World Wars'** website, I noticed the name of Albert John Broadfield. This interested me because of my relation Les Broadfield. I contacted Vicky to make her aware of this article of Albert, born in Bridgnorth on 5 July 1876, the son of Sarah and Richard Broadfield. Albert married Rebecca Wilkes at St Mary's Church in 1898 and 20 years later enlisted in the Royal Army Medical Corps. During the First World War he was also a special constable in

Wolverhampton. Due to his age of 42, I should imagine that this was prior to his posting in Carlisle at Fusehill War Hospital; discharged in 1919.

Before going into my short writing titled 'My Heath Town Hike,' let me explain as to why I have posted it on this Facebook page. Reason being is that there is a mention of playing football on Heath Town Park; the year was 1986 and I remember quite clearly as that was the year that my dad died.

We were in the process of moving into Codsall and when doing so it was obvious that there was a great local Wolverhampton Sunday League involvement and interest in the area. I have a sporting background and had been taking time off to run marathons; 10 to be exact. I was by now in my thirties and got asked to sign for Codsall Bull football team; it was on the pub garden actually and I was there with my two children. I was astonished by the amount of supporters that followed the football team. The Village Hall pitch was lined with many spectators; I believe the first away game was at Heath Town Park; to be honest you good folk of Codsall impressed me greatly. Coincidently the person who took his football boots off at half-time for me to play is Tony Doody. He is related to Terry Baker, my brother-in-law, and from the Doody family who had the paper shop on Bilston Street. Gareth delivered papers for them and I often helped him. The Doodys also used to be on Steelhouse Lane by the Why Knot pub.

A Wulfrunian Way

MY HEATH TOWN HIKE; Thoughts went back to when Lynne told me that she knew it was me by my walk. She was waiting for me near our guest house in Broughty Ferry, Scotland. It was before breakfast that I had caught the early bus to Dundee to walk back again as near as possible to the Tay. This was a link to my coastal walk that I needed to do, but as said she knew it was me. It may be different on this particular day as I had a walking stick with me (recovering from back surgery) and painkillers so I can walk from New Cross Hospital, where she works, to town. I was driving into the hospital with her to hike back to home. "You must be mad, "she told me, "I wish you wasn't, but be careful."

Plans were to have my breakfast of a couple of apples on the gardens of St Peter's Church. I cut through Heath Town Park and stopped for a while to look at the frosty football pitch. I can recall playing my first away game for Codsall Bull in 1986. As said earlier, I was impressed with how many supporters followed a pub team! Also I was in the area of my old workmate Len Muir, sadly gone now. He lived on Prestwood Road and we had great days at Delta in the early 1970's.

Before leaving Heath Town I called in at Holy Trinity Church and walked on the frosty green grass of the graveyard where some of my ancestors are at rest. Earlier this year I had been directed to Sampson Darby and his wife Sarah Wheaton, just to name two.

Out by the old Heath Town Baths and across the busy junction. Youngsters were chatting and making their way to relevant schools. It was noticeable of the calming atmosphere when canal side. Signage for the city centre soon came and within a few minutes I had arrived at St Peter's gardens at 9.00am where an apple and a paracetamol was my breakfast. I rested there absorbing a few minutes of Friday morning. It became a '1964 world' and I was ten years old, following instructions to meet a teacher by the fountain early Saturday morning as I had been selected for All Saints Junior School football team. It was early Friday morning in my now '2018 world' and I was not expecting anyone to come for me.

I needed to get home to Codsall, I had made a promise to Lynne that I wouldn't be walking too far so it was a train journey back. I had almost an hour wait so I browsed about looking at the new development without failing to notice the changes. The very sign of Queen Street took me to where we got on and off the number 30 bus to Rough Hills. The Army Recruitment building with the Union Flag lying low waiting for wind like a racehorse for water.

My train pulled away without delay at 10.25am; I was sitting in a backward facing seat; buildings gradually grew faint; Wolverhampton is changing around me, just as it did for my Wulfrunian ancestors.

(13) **My Heath Town Hike** ©

My Heath Town hike on Friday
took me back in my day,
tied are priceless memories
in Kennedy Tartan ribbons,
I seem to carry them along,
each and every single word
adds to a loving living song.
I'm never skint,
my Scottish Wulfrunian footprint;
my wealth's on shore and ground,
wherever I leave them around.

EATING MY HEART OUT IN EASTFIELD; Do you
remember that time Rob when you was outside of Ladybank Primary School in Fife, Scotland? That's a question I asked myself, as I recalled the time when I was looking at where my dad had been educated. The school was built in 1890 and on its website these days is that 'it serves the village of Ladybank along with the outlying hamlets of Edenstown and Giffordtown plus several farms and isolated homes.' That itself could describe school day life in my dad's time in the 1930's.

My imaginative mind would've been on full power as I mined deep to unearth genealogy information. There was also a comparison of his schooling and mine and where and how I spent my young years? If my research is correct Wolverhampton Archives & Local studies state that the Eastfield School, where I was taught in my secondary years, opened in 1870.

A well worn phrase of mine 'those who follow my writing' will be familiar with my work inspired by walks about Wolverhampton, Codsall and Scotland. So once again 'those who follow my writing' will know that I am also following something that is my physiotherapists advice to 'keep moving' because of a problem I have at the moment.

All the above had led me to be outside of Eastfield; a school building that educated the Victorian, Edwardian and modern eras of children; one of them being me.

As I had last week, 'those who follow my writing' (be careful not to over use this phrase old boy) will know that I had travelled in with Lynne to work at New Cross Hospital to do some walking somewhere different than the streets of Codsall, which I do most days. The idea this time was to get the old legs going and take-in part of the Eastfield area that grew familiar to me in the mid to late 60's.

A Wulfrunian Way

The mind travels further than man, well that's what I think. Looking back on this week alone; with a proud feeling of family; I was in the audience at both Perton and Shareshill, as grandad, watching nativity plays, that take me back more than a hundred and also a couple of thousand years if you think about it religiously. Yesterday was the final school run of the year, a granddaughter and myself singing loudly in the car to "Last Christmas, I gave you my heart."

On the day that the world introduced me to Eastfield School, I had walked past Chillington works where my bloodline grandfather Benjamin James Owen worked and was also a goalkeeper in their football team. At the time family history around Wolverhampton or Scotland didn't play as an important part in my life as it does now. Eastfield seemed miles away from my 'Rough Hills world' and truth is as an eleven year old, for my immediate future I did feel different as many fellow pupils were from streets and roads that I had never heard of.

From the building of the former Eastfield school, I looked over to the corner at Cross Street where I would've walked around in 1965 to see it as a pupil for the first time. For a moment I expected to see me doing so again. I waited a while but as expected, that lad in his new school uniform didn't show. I crossed over the busy road for the opposite view. The Friday traffic travelled up and down the Willenhall Road, the 64 year old man did so as well; contented about thinking of those days.

Time to set off and head for the station as once again, I have a train to Codsall to catch. All around there is change but the boy in me hasn't. For a start St Matthew's Church isn't there any more at the junction of Walsall Street and Horseley Fields. I should imagine that without the housing about these parts no more there wasn't a need for it. How sad that the one time places of importance are wiped off the landscape. I thought of mom's cousin Ricky who worked at BOC which is still there. This road for me was strange as it was much more quiet than it was in my younger days

I chose to walk the Lower Walsall Street way towards town (still like to call it that even though we have city status). A short while later I was to be close to my Owen and Williams family street name addresses that I have of the past. Also the long gone places of work where employment was needed for families to be fed. Just as I do in Fife and Dundee; whilst absorbed in thought, I walked the roads and streets of my ancestors.

A thirteen year old lad in 1967 turned into Commercial Road, making his way through All Saints to Rough Hills. The sixty-four year old man of 2018 didn't; he had a train to catch at the ever changing Wolverhampton Railway Station.

One last find was Duke Street where my maternal grandmother was born. She didn't live long enough for my mother and of course myself to know her. "C'mon Rob, get walking now, let's get that train."

(14) **Eating My Heart Out in Eastfield** ©

"Time to walk the old roads,
aye, the growing-up old, old roads;
walk the dear old, old roads, one more time. "
"I'll meet you in the old streets
your streets, your old streets,
come and greet me in the old streets,
the dear old, old streets."
"I'm never skint,
my Scottish Wulfrunian footprint;
my wealth's on shore and ground,
wherever I leave them around."

A Wulfrunian Way

A Wulfrunian Way

MY CHRISTMAS WISH OF A STORY; A family get together with Grannie Rowley, far left, in picture. There's me at the front in my Christmas jumper.

'A get-together, those jolly social gatherings, where cousins meet their extended family.' Those lines of mine from an earlier poem of mine. On one of those photographs of special occasions is an uncle of ours that we knew as Hotch. I would be very young at the time but I do know that sadly he lost his life in a motorcycle accident. He was married to Aunt Jan, and because of my age I have little recollection of him other than being the tallest in a photograph taken one Christmas at our house on Rough Hills. 'Hotch,' real name Brian Cartwright, was in the navy, and I found out that he brought Gareth and myself a reversible, zip-up jacket each from abroad. One winter he was to build a snowman with us - apparently as a joke he said that we had put him off kids! Aunt Jan later married Michael Langford. Uncle Mick was into photography and recordings, taking great pleasure in later years of showing me that I had been caught again pulling a face at the camera.

I can't help but think of Christmas's past. In recent years, in the festive season, Gareth, Stuart and myself meet in a Wolverhampton pub for a drink. It would've been great for our dad to be with us but sadly, to old age he never got there. Our own individual plans have probably already been arranged and mom would've known if it's Gareth's or my turn to have her as a guest for Christmas dinner. Incidentally, in our childhood days, our tree and decorations did not go up until Christmas Eve.

The evenings, when we were growing up was always spent celebrating with family. Christmas and Boxing Day evenings was at our house or Aunt Shirl and Uncle Bill's or Aunt Jan and Uncle Mick's. I recall that my uncles Mick

and Bill also having their mothers joining us. 'Put and Take,'
a game I found that first became known during the First
World War, was always the enjoyable family entertainment
of the night. If I recall correctly the spinner was Uncle Bill's.
The original 6 x sided spinners were made from bullets by
soldiers in the trenches. (This is in Jayne's possession).

     Uncle Bill, like his namesake William Duncombe the
English composer (ca.1736 — 30 November 1818) was an
accomplished pianist. He was always the one at family
parties to entertain musically. One was at the Butlers Arms
when Fred and Barb Lavender kept it. Trouble was the piano
was downstairs and the party upstairs! It was 'hands on' to
move the heavy musical instrument - with me watching
from the back and my dad, a step or two down, laughing his
head-off! He also played the organ at St Andrew's Church in
Whitmore Reans and Bushbury Crematorium. I can recall
seeing a photograph of him in the Express and Star as he
was playing the piano for a dance class performance. Uncle
Bill's musical talent appears to have been passed down in
his family as their name of Duncombe is often popping-up
playing live somewhere. A poem of mine titled 'My Uncle
Bill' is in my first book 'On a Wolverhampton Journey.'

     I could stake a claim with inspiring my cousin
Michael to pick up and play the stringed musical instrument.
There's a family photograph by a Christmas tree, he has one
arm around our cousin Liane and his other around me with
my Elvis Presley guitar.

A Wulfrunian Way

(15) **My Christmas Wish of a Story** ©

Thankful that I've shared mom's old age
experienced that love she has of family,
countless stories for her sons to store
often heard and always more,
pleased that I've shared mom's old age
but dad...he never got there.
A pleasant time on Christmas Eve
Great Western, Wolverhampton
two ordinary looking customers
my elder brother and me,
he spends time in France
that short crossing o'er the sea,
me, I'm quite at home in Scotland
Fifeshire and Dundee.
At a table for two in the conservatory part
afternoon light was shining through,
visibility of the outside, ay there was that too.
"Our great grandfather on the Owen side"
I told, "died in Sun Street, fifty yards from here,"
mixed the conversation we did with family history
amongst the break-up festive cheer,
he with a glass of cider, me a Guinness beer.
Railways and canals, buildings,
lost works and old pals,
two elderly men mulling o'er a nostalgic pint
that's what we're like, a laddie once again was I
with the elder bro' who fixed my bike.
We spoke of ailments that we had,
Wolverhampton and of Scotland
and of course our mom and dad.
On the afternoon of Christmas Eve
up the cobbles of Corn Hill we went,
time spent, more often....ay we should
in the course of brotherhood.

A Wulfrunian Way

He went his way, I went mine,
Great Western, Wolverhampton,
a couple of hours of sociable time
I'd say we both appreciated:
to the railway station there I stood and waited,
aye I waited once again for an outbound train.
The outbound train, the outbound train
that I wish was inbound!
Inbound to younger days in Wolverhampton.
Without being considered ungrateful;
extremely thankful that I've shared mom's old age
experienced that love she always has of family,
countless stories for her sons to store
often heard and always more,
pleased that I've shared mom's old age
but dad.....he never got there;
stories, my Christmas wish of a story.

A Wulfrunian Way

ANDY STEWART SANG ON HOGMANAY; Half-way into my early morning walk around Codsall; approaching Birches Bridge to be exact. A lorry passes me on route to a well known store; closely followed by a brewery wagon. It's Hogmanay 2019 and preparations to celebrate the new year will soon be started. News on TV earlier shows that Edinburgh is already under way. I carried on towards the village, turning at Histons Hill lights and down to Sandy Lane. All was quiet and dark around St Nicholas Church. I could see that the flag – assuming it is St George's - was blowing in the Hogmanay wind. I recalled how my childhood house was on this day.

(16) **Andy Stewart Sang on Hogmanay** ©

Our childhood house was merry
on the night of New Years Eve.
Andy Stewart sang on Hogmanay
kilted ladies danced the year away,
all were joyful on the night of New Years Eve.
Our childhood house was merry
on the night of New Years Eve.
My parents were radiant with joy,
aye they were in the eyes of this wee boy.
There were friendly neighbour wishes,
shaking of hands and kisses,
all were joyful on the night of New Years Eve.
Our childhood house was merry
on the night of New Years Eve.
Andy Stewart sang on Hogmanay
kilted ladies danced the year away,
aye, Jock's hoose was lood an' cantie
on the night of New Years Eve.

A Wulfrunian Way

1
Sweet Mary, Will You Wait With Me to See Lucy ©
Robbie Kennedy Bennett

(17) **Sweet Mary,**
Will You Wait With Me to See Lucy ©

It was in the year of 1857
Benjamin Owen and Mary Farnell they married
at the church of St John's, Wolverhampton
on a day in November;
I believe it was a Monday if the facts are right.
Benjamin and sweet Mary, how I foresaw
both with a loving smile, when walking down the aisle
on your wedding day in November.
Benjamin, your father was a miner from Hanley Green
Mary, yours from Wheaton Aston,
each a Staffordshire grafter
imagine the working class laughter,
but oh,15 years after
tears the children cried when poor Mary died.
Families, illness, less chance of recovery
pre-20th century medical discovery,
all having an affect on hard living, tough times.
Rough Hills colliery one can assume
is where the mines were being excavated,
many I am related to earned a living on this side of town.
Oh Mary, poor Mary, born in Union Street
and in Bilston Road at the young age of thirty
you were called, I am appalled that you were called.
What I shall do Mary Farnell sweet Mary Farnell
is visit the church of St John's, Wolverhampton;
I will wait outside and see you come outside
a young and happy, smiling beautiful bride,
oh Mary Farnell sweet Mary Farnell.
Mary, sweet Mary
it was in the year of 1883
that your son Isaiah Owen and Lucy Wardley married

A Wulfrunian Way

at the church of St John's, Wolverhampton
on a day in August;
I believe it was a Monday if the facts are right,
but oh, imagine 18 years later
tears children cried when poor Lucy died.
Also for Lucy, dearest Lucy,
I will wait outside and see her come outside
a young and happy, smiling beautiful bride,
and Mary, sweet Mary, please will you wait there with me?

A Wulfrunian Way

Praise the Skilled Men of the Georgian Era ©
Robbie Kennedy Bennett

(18) **Praise the Skilled Men of the Georgian Era** ©

Buildings that you are familiar with
places that you know well,
you believe you did, thought you did
stopped looking you did you can tell.
A reason to get up closer to
with time to give some thought
December sun, colourful stone it brought out
the sense of sight of my photographic eye
'an interesting picture could be caught.'
Praise the skilled men of that era
you guys set the level high,
soon to be inside of this Georgian work
as the afternoon time is ticking on by.
The Church of St John's in the Square
a sad reason to come brought me there,
Wolverhampton's second oldest church, a true fact
unprepared how my mind would react.
Back to 1760 and the first congregation
in a somewhat imaginative rural setting,
the towns population expanding
more industrial about to be getting.
Surroundings, horses and carriages
funerals, christenings and marriages,
they all in some way 'tip toed' through
the mind of this man as they often do.
The welcome December sun did seem
make the stonework an interestingly sandy cream,
is it a history visit of mine
back into old Wulfrunian time?
Praise the skilled men of the Georgian era
and condolences this modern, incomparable day,

I listened respectively and thoughtfully
of their loved one and his final journey,
I heard questions they asked of Jesus
and his answer that "he is the way."
I was a child of this town again, a boy and youth,
a strict but good upbringing, a man of principles
always speaking the truth.
Buildings that I am familiar with
places that I know well,
I believed I did, thought I did
stopped looking I did I could tell.

(19) I'd Be Fifteen At The Time ©

During a picture gallery browsing
a journey I'm taken on
days, months and years have gone
a journey worthwhile
Nostalgia that's my style
I'd be fifteen at the time
she visited this church and garden in 1969
the Queen Mother when she came to Wolverhampton
at The Royal School she unveiled a commemorative plaque
and Clarence House declared it open
'she was presented with a brooch
in the shape of a Staffordshire Knot'
above was interesting research
after discovering the stone at St John's Church
in St John's Square in the garden leisurely looking there
Back to when I was fifteen at the time
when she visited this church and garden in 1969
I'd be leaving school starting work earning wages
into my book of life relatively early pages
different directions I made starting way back then
travelled many a mile

Nostalgia that's my style
now I'm referred to as an 'old age pensioner'
and my reflection confirms I'm well worn
further on in my book of life
now a little shabby and pages torn
obvious ageing skin and bone
weathered just like that stone
But I'd be fifteen at the time
she visited this church and garden in 1969
the Queen Mother when she came to Wolverhampton
She married at Westminster Abbey in 1923
and I see that she laid her wedding bouquet
on the Tomb of the Unknown Warrior
coming into being a royal tradition
apparently in public the 'first modern royal to smile'
in her very own gracious style

I NEVER KNEW HIM AS GRANDAD;

There's a photograph or two that I often see of recruits assembling outside of Wolverhampton Town Hall in 1914. Many of those men were to leave Wolverhampton and not return. My real grandfather Benjamin James Owen did return but as a casualty. I have often wondered if he is on one of those photographs but 'Recruits For Kitchener's Army Leaving Wolverhampton was August 29th 1914. Upon checking with his war records, his signing up was 11th December 1915 therefore not so. Nevertheless he or some of our family could have been in the crowd watching those brave fellows going off to war. In the festive period of 2019 when in Wolverhampton, I took a photo of the Town Hall, thinking of that time.

The Battle of Arras; according to my Uncle Ben's letter is the battle where Benjamin James Owen, 4th Lincolnshire Regiment, suffered his injuries on 25th April 1917 escaping as a POW.

It's early on the 3rd day of 2019 and I am thinking of my bloodline grandad, all because I have noticed a video posted on the Band of the Royal Regiment of Scotland

Facebook page back in May 2018; 'Today's Thursday throwback looks at our involvement in the centenary of the Battle of Arras commemorations. What a privilege it was to perform in the same square that 100 years previously had seen a military band performing to the soldiers who would soon take part in the Battle of Arras.' '100 years on, please join us to honour Britain's bravest... past and present.' 'Get your tickets and CD for our 'Walking With Heroes' tour.'

     Pictured overleaf is Benjamin James Owen and Sarah Ann Owen (nee Williams) with their first child Benjamin Joseph Owen.

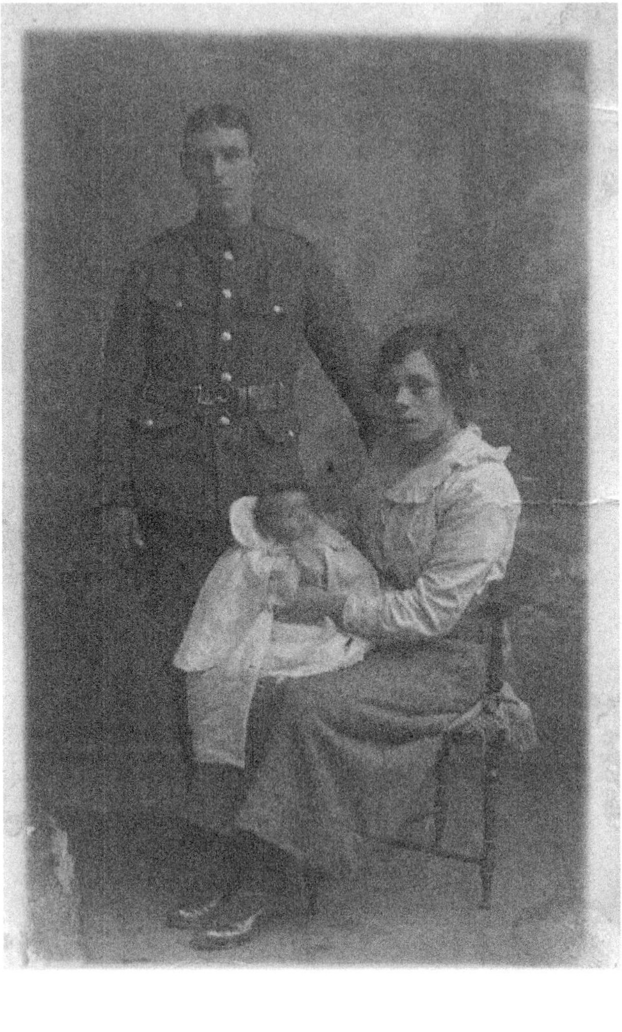

(20) I Never Knew Him as Grandad ©

I never knew him as grandad
I loved him, who stood in his place,
I grew up without understanding
Not thinking to picture his face.
In a time of worries and troubles
An age of conflict and war,
Who is the man in the photo?
To my thoughts I open the door.
His regiment was the 4TH Lincoln's
Held captive but made his escape,
Wounded by a bullet in a shoulder
Desperate and in poor shape.
The battlefield he crawled for four days
Drinking water from bottles of dead,
French Officers saw movement in a body
Injured by bullets of lead.
Discharged in 1918
In his regiment he could no longer be,
He was no longer physically able
A young man of just twenty-three.
He lived on to be forty-one
But pneumonia set in and he died,
I never knew him as grandad
Then inside a part of me cried.

Because of my writing I have received many interesting messages; one came from Derek Mills, also growing up in Cheviot Road. He also wanted to write a book about Rough Hills, which proved to be very popular when published. We continued to keep in contact. Another book that he is co-author of is 'All Saints at War,' in which Benjamin James Owen is mentioned.

A Wulfrunian Way

THE CALLING OF TIME BY BARB AND FRED LAVENDER;

The answer to my question was, "yes we have, a grey one." I had been retracing where I had been and suddenly thought of the petrol station in Perton. After finding their phone number I gave them a call and asked if anyone had handed in a hat?

It all came together when I recalled where I had been for petrol. It was in Perton where I have grandchildren living, and where I am there during school term doing school run and pick-ups. Perton wasn't there in my growing up years so it was new to me; due to the fact that I live in Codsall it is now quite local to me.

The day before my 'lost hat day' was New Years Day 2019. Roads are quiet as I drive towards Bentley Bridge; so quiet that the family history mind is so active that it warms me with gladness and sadness that is totally acceptable. This being so as I had passed by where The Squirrel public house used to be. This was one of the few pubs that Fred and Barb Lavender were licensees. I can recall one Christmas when a family party was held in the room at the back. A few minutes earlier I had drove by the Butlers Arms, another pub of theirs, once again memories of many a family get together.

(21) **The Calling of Time by Barb or Fred Lavender** ©

Visitors, in the living room,
old-fashioned fireplaces and grates,
ornaments and wallpaper
takes me back to the fifties and sixties;
maturing into the seventies,
pleasantries I presume;
feature or factor,

A Wulfrunian Way

likeable character or two in the living room.
You know I can't go around Wolverhampton much
without a kindred feeling, allied by blood and partnership
togetherness in a home of relatedness.
Take the time when I am driving down Bushbury Road,
where The Squirrel used to be,
awareness of Barb and Fred Lavender
family history and memories mean everything to me.
We go on our way doing things that we have to do
living our every day, turning negativity into positivity,
rich without having a pocket full of money
family history and memories mean everything to me.
Take the time when driving up Elston Hall Lane
same feeling again, negotiating the traffic island
into Kempthorne Avenue; I'm certain,
conscious of opening a memory curtain
significantly the Butlers Arms will be there
I 'll see that pair; Barb and Fred Lavender.
You know I can't go around Wolverhampton much
without remembering merriment,
a kindred spiritual experiment
appears to be some how comparable.
Same when I'm in Wolverhampton
near the 'Man on the Oss,' in Queen Square,
I hear the calling of "time,"
in the infamous Tavern in the Town
by Barb or Fred Lavender.
Other public houses that regulars may raise
and always, Barb and Fred Lavender
will be named, life is a picture, keep it framed
so I can see, obviously because
family history and memories mean everything to me.
I can't go around Wolverhampton much
without thinking of places, people and faces,
dwellings, children laughing and yelling;

public houses, kept alive in this rhyme,
still heard is the calling of "time"
which echoes loudly, coming from that family of mine.
Looking through childhood eyes
at visitors, for a while
in the old-style living room.

'I remember them all, the Tavern in the Town was my favourite, I've got lot's of happy memories of staying with Deb in the school holidays.' (Jo Eagleton)
     Overleaf is a picture of Fred Lavender and Barbara Allen's wedding.

A Wulfrunian Way

RECEIVED FROM Stewart Lavender;
Hi Robbie, As per your facebook message, I thought I would give you some information about the Lavender side of things. However, I don't know a lot about my Grandparents Fred and Barbara (although I would like to know more).

    I'll start with me, I am the only child of Mark Frederick Lavender born in October 1950. When I was born in February 1978, I was taken home to a flat on Tipton Road in Sedgley, I believe this residence has been converted back to a large house these days. In May of 78 we moved to Lomond Road on the Northway estate in Sedgley. My parents didn't move away from that address until mother moved approximately one year after father's death. She still resides on the Northway estate. I lived in Penn Common for a couple of years before moving to Warstones for 4 years and then on to Shifnal where I have been for the last 3 years.

    Father died in 2007 from Lung Cancer. It was a relatively short illness. From what I can remember about my dad's working life it was mainly spent at a company in Darlaston called Altas Bolt. He spent approximately 19years here before the company went into liquidation. He worked as a foreman in the heat treatment department. Strangely I now work in the same industry and only half a mile from dad's place of work. After Atlas bolt he worked for a company in Wednesbury called Eurofast Petrochemical Supplies. He was at Eurofast until he died. As things go it turns out that I have ended up working for the same company although the company has now changed name to Lonestar Fasteners Europe.

    Dad was a keen fisherman and loved to watch all sports especially Football and Cricket. Dad had a brother and sister; Nick and Deborah. I'm not sure where Nick lives now, I believe it to be Tettenhall. Deborah lives out in the countryside near to Bridgnorth in a place called Stableford.

As mentioned I know little about Fred & Barbara. I remember their time at the Fisherman in Wednesfield before they moved to the Yew Tree in Graisley. When they retired, they moved to Third Avenue in Low Hill. I remember Grandad running the Hockey Club on Wobaston Road, Pendeford where Wolves used to train. I remember being privileged enough to go and watch them train. Seeing David Kelly playing in goal instead of practising shooting and meeting so many of my heroes. I also recall a story of Grandad giving Graham Taylor a massive rollocking for the players leaving the changing room in a right state. I couldn't believe what he had done, I mean Graham Taylor, Wolves and ex-England manager!

I've heard of stories of Grandad's pubs, Tavern in the Town, Butlers Arms, Pear Tree and I think the Squirrel. I'm sure there were more that I am unaware of.

Nick Lavender has three sons, Nick, Neil and Dean. Nick the eldest lives in Wombourne and is now in the pub trade himself. Neil lives in Tettenhall and Dean is also in Wombourne. Debbie has a daughter called Lucy who lives near to Leamington Spa after growing up near Bantock Park and Finchfield. I don't know anything about Nan and Grandad's parents or even where they were both born. I don't even know if they had brothers or sister although I would imagine that they had some siblings as we are related in one way or another because of this. If you have any information on Nan or Grandad's upbringings, I would be interested to hear about it. I hope that I have not gone on too much or moved off topic. Good luck with your new book, I hope it is a success. (Stewart Lavender)

OUR SHAZ, THE FRIENDLIEST ANGEL IN HEAVEN; In the kitchen cooking and listening to the radio and Diana Ross's voice sings out and I think of our Shaz, the friendliest angel in heaven. I would love to turn time back many years to see you in our living room turning conversation a humorous way. A reminder from Diana Ross that 'Our Shaz' is still in the family.

This takes me back to a Monday evening in February 1980 and Lynne had been visiting Aunt Mill's house on Thompson Avenue. Lynne was driving a black Mini Clubman GT at the time that the sales manager of our next car snapped up because of the low mileage. Shaz hadn't long had Amber and Lynne was expecting our first child. The same time next evening we were the proud parents for the first time as Marie was born that morning. Aunt Mill 'insisted' that it was because of the cheese and brown sauce sandwich that Shaz made!

A Wulfrunian Way

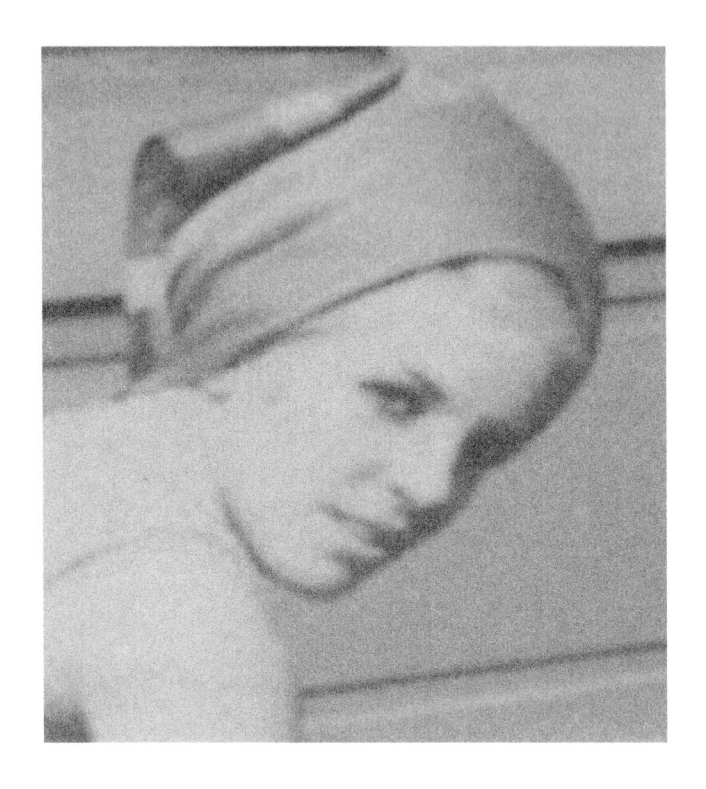

(22) **Our Shaz,
the Friendliest Angel in Heaven** ©

Our Shaz
was vibrant and funny
with a personality
as sweet as honey
good company was she
our Shaz
Our Shaz...
she's an angel now,
our Shaz
the friendliest angel in heaven
that will be our Shaz

RECEIVED FROM Dee Weaver; Hey Robbie, My name is Deirdre Helen, aka DeeDee, dad only calls me Deirdre if I'm in trouble. I was born Nov 1961 at 7 Thompson Ave to Eric (Ricky) and Ellen Hodgetts (nee O'Keeffe) and I was the first grandchild of Mill and Ernie, lived with nan and grand until I was about 4 then moved. I have a younger Sister Annette or Netty (I call her Nitty) and 2 younger bros Steve and Ian, we had a lovely childhood growing up on Ashmore Park. I have a son Jay who is 34 and I now live in New Invention, work for the City Council and love getting together with family. That's me in a very little nutshell. (Author note; Ricky was one of 20,000 British servicemen deployed to Kiritimati, known as Christmas Island, for nuclear tests).

DELTA; The Delta factory was on the Bilston Road, Monmore Green, formerly E.P. Jenks Ltd. Mr. E. P. Jenks had taken over the original firm Hyde & Co, in 1918, which itself was formed in 1873. Starting off as washer and small pressed work makers and water fittings, in 1969 when I started there they were extruding brass and copper from billets. I have to admit that during my days there I was spoilt rotten! All because my mother was the canteen manageress and Aunt Mill, Wendy and Sharon also worked there. It was a good job that I was into football and running as when it came to food I had preferential treatment.

There was some happy days at Delta, making some good friends, such as Terry Yates in the toolroom and Fred Lambert on maintenance. Terry was one of a few there who played football. So did Mick and Derek Lee out of central works. Fred and I sometimes had a pint in the Monkey House on a Saturday dinner time after work. He also took a great interest in following me playing football.

Every time I go by that way so much jumps out at me. None more so than the office and canteen buildings, still there from 1937. It makes me want to walk in there once more and be spoilt again by Aunt Mill, Wend and Shaz.

THE TAVERN TO ME IS STILL STANDING.....;

"Keep up the good work" said Shirley; While heading towards Queen Square today I bumped into Shirley Preston Whenever there's a question about Rough Hills Shirley always copies me in to see if I can help. "Keep up the good work" said Shirley, it was kind of her to encourage me to keep writing.

I had walked from the train station to Queen Square then out of town towards Rough Hills. It's all changed since my youthful days as the ABC was still there in this old mind of mine. Cleveland Street was a busy road back then. I looked up at a window in The Royal Hospital and for a second caught sight of me waving at me! A patient there a few times I have been because of my active sporting past.

On Steelhouse Lane I was trying to work out where the scrapyard was that dad and Percy Piddock worked in. All Saints Church and school always draw my attention.

Granny Williams's house on the corner of

Steelhouse Lane and Major Street has been gone for many years now. Nevertheless it still activates this mind of mine. Monkey House is no more and the MEB no longer comes into view. I paused for a short while and studied the factory wall that is industrially artistic. Built by hard working bricklayers of the past.

Later, back at the station, a train pulled in to take passengers to Liverpool. One thinks if there is someone heading home, just as I have.

In addition to my previous writing of the gathering of green space around West Park, East Park, Dixon Street, Rooker Avenue and Bantock Park. As a child you may think that things shall stay the same forever; not giving a thought for the future and that they may not. As a boy born in the 1950's, obviously Rough Hills and how it was back then is prominently set in my mind. I paused a few times to take in the area as it is now, on this February day of 2017.

Somewhat cold but bright and sunny giving a good feeling to be out walking in the fresh air. Now a man in my 60's, the atmosphere was very different. All that I can put it down to is that we must have been an active, outdoor generation in those days.

In one diagonal photograph that I take of the playing fields; for a second or two the tavern is still there. In fact a branch on a tree points to the very place where it was. An imaginary football match is being played and a forward has had a shot at goal. He has missed the target by a good distance and the ball was bouncing around the pub car park. Kids jump off the wall and are scampering about to boot it back.

I made my way back to my car which I had parked on Rooker Avenue, by where there was once an air raid shelter. I had taken photographs of the mosaics on the wall in the close where The Rough Hills Tavern was. I craved for the old days; in reality I was being selfish as this is now other people's home and is now their day.

Suddenly my mind went back even further to when the area was known to have mines. In fact on my Wolverhampton side I have found that I descend from a miner named Samuel Williams born in the 1800's with a birthplace of Rough Hills. My, it must have been unrecognisable before the housing and only the odd cottages scattered around. If it was possible for us to be here together on this day, a history lesson there to behold and to ease my longing.

I eventually got into my car, turned around, pulled away and drove past Rooker Avenue shops. Another Williams relation of mine owned two of them when first built. Before then he had a hut on Dixon Street playing fields. Time to go Rough Hills laddie, your mind's over working, it's all over for now, time to go.

(23) The Tavern To Me is Still Standing Over There ©

Was a day of time spent outside for self therapy
re-visiting places that hold my bygone years,
tears and longing came calling from the inside
the future has contents that the past does not prepare
the tavern to me is still standing over there.
The tavern to me is still standing over there
children are playing, playing over there,
staying, staying, staying young and fair
the present has contents of the past that's everywhere
as the tavern to me is still standing over there.

A TRIBUTE TO NAN AND GRANDAD;

A position of a good height on a January day of 2019 gifted to me a pleasant view into Shropshire. On this well used ipad of mine, from Bushbury Crematorium, I zoomed in to the Wrekin. It wasn't a crystal clear day and better photographs will be found if you go surfing the internet. Yes the Wrekin, been up there I have and last time it was with Xena our Staffie. Trees I must add that I was looking down on and over reminded me of Fife. Feelings were, is that I don't come here as much as I should do. Peaceful and thoughtful, just as I prefer sometimes, it weakens and strengthens me, hurts and mends. I looked down once again to read George Rowley, also his wife Jane; names of my nan and grandad. It wasn't a crystal clear day but quite explicit was my feelings of loving those two people very dearly. With regard to my poem, a pleasant surprise came my way when I found that Uncle Eddy was so impressed that he had painted and framed it.

A Wulfrunian Way

A TRIBUTE TO NAN AND GRANDAD

BY ROBBIE BENNETT

My Grandad was a quiet man,
but still liked family around,
While Nan sat there talking
he'd hardly say a sound.
Sitting in his armchair,
Hearing others talk,
Never ever offending
Often liked to walk.
I can see him in his suit and tie,
Looking neat and smart.
My Grandad was a quiet man,
with the biggest kindest heart

My Nan she always told stories
of the old days and years gone by.
She must have been a young rascal,
I could tell by that glint in her eye.
The cheekiest grin on a lady
Will never be seen no more.
I'm sure up in Heaven God's smiling,
Since Jane Rowley has passed through His door.

George and Jane Rowley
of Steelhouse Lane
Wolverhampton

(24) A TRIBUTE TO NAN AND GRANDAD ©
George and Jane Rowley

My Grandad was a quiet man
But still liked family around.
While Nan sat there talking
He'd hardly say a sound.
Sitting in his armchair
Hearing others talk,
Never ever offending
Often liked to walk.
I can see him in his suit and tie
Looking neat and smart,
My Grandad was a quiet man
With the biggest kindest heart.

My Nan she always told stories
Of the old days and years gone by,
She must have been a young rascal
I can tell by that look in her eye.
The cheekiest grin on a lady
Will never be seen no more,
I'm sure up in heaven God's smiling
Since Jane Rowley has passed through his door.

SARAH ANN AND THE SEPTEMBER SKY; This piece of writing below is taken from my first book **Awa' th' Rough Hills an' Awa'**;
I wrote this with careful consideration of the two people I consider of being my Grandparents. My brothers and myself loved them wholeheartedly. Sad circumstances concerning

our maternal grandmother but love overcome of which we are thankful. Sarah Ann, died within weeks of our mother's birth.

On another note, on the first day of September 2013, at the time of writing, the sky was a colourful delight. Coincidently it was also noticed by a cousin of mine (Mick Duncombe) who had posted some stunning photographs on his Facebook page.

(25) **Sarah Ann and the September Sky** ©

September sky
Striking it is, oh why?
As I try to write of, Sarah Ann
A Sunday light blue
And I'm writing of you
A Sunday light blue, Sarah Ann, I can see
As the evening draws in, gradually
Fifty nine summers so far
Fifty nine summers
None shared with Sarah Ann
My maternal Gran, Sarah Ann
A father of two I became
Feels good to tell you and write your name
Bloodline, from the same
Aren't we Sarah Ann?
Fifty nine summers
Fifty nine summers, Sarah Ann, I have had
Four children call me Grandad
And for your daughter, my mother, I am glad
Sarah Ann, your story is sad
Motherhood, a premature end
Your six children couldn't comprehend
From newborn up to aged eleven
Asking why, their mother, had to go to heaven?

A Wulfrunian Way

A mother of three boys, your baby daughter became
Feels good to tell you and write your name
Into my mind you came
My maternal Gran, Sarah Ann
We missed you Sarah Ann
In the passing of time
Now, Sarah Ann
You are sharing these minutes of mine
September sky
Amazing, why oh why?
As the sky is red Sarah Ann
And now, a Sunday dark blue
A Sunday dark blue
As I'm writing of you
A Sunday dark blue, Sarah Ann I have said
Is it you in that September sky, that September red?
That September red, Sarah Ann I have said
If true, Sarah Ann, if true
My fifty ninth summer
... Then I've shared this summer with you!

SHE'S SOMEWHERE NEAR; I've been told many times before that my writing that leads to books is greatly influenced by family and the very person that I am. Each and every one of those who I descend from I give credit to, even if only by thought and if possible by word. Today I spent time at Merridale Cemetery, Jeffcock Road. I cleaned leaves away from a plaque in one final resting place and looked at another and saw nothing, which made me think and write of something that was a lot more than everything, and 'I think, I'll write of you...right here.'

(26) She's Somewhere Near ©
I never knew her,
she's at rest around about here.
Sad circumstances,
she's at rest around about here.
Wolverhampton times were extremely hard,

her short life I shan't discard.
Sad circumstances, has said, no other,
blood related, then she's my grandmother.
There's nowhere to read her name,
but still I feel good that I came.
We missed many a time to celebrate,
'cause of by blood we relate.
Such as blessings for the new year,
Sarah Ann, I feel you're somewhere near,
as I think and write of you, Sarah Ann;
I think and write of you...right here.

(27) **My Story** ©

No need to go too far and to think too deep,
we were a band of brothers dreaming football in our sleep.
We didn't know it then but we knew when
time was time and now's the time for the football field
Now we must be grey or balding old men
to battle our own survival
Where's the muscle gone from these legs
how come my waistline has increased,
the beast of ageing has attacked
my defence has lacked and leaked
There's ten thousand and more better poets than me,
but they don't tell my story
a verse of my story
To the guys who built the steeples
the lassie's who served the stores,
and those who fought the two world wars
created freedom in my story
Where's the hair gone from this head
the muscle gone from this frame,
what does remain
is my name in my story

A Wulfrunian Way

Hard going in old Wulfrunian times
trousers turned up and sowing,
I'm supposing you've heard my Scottish tail
that I descend from a family named Traill
in my story, my Scottish story
There's twenty thousand and more better poets than me,
but they don't tell my story,
a rhyming line of my story
See that house there, well that is where
my grandparents did live in Low Hill
and still I consider that they influence my story
A six year old grandson runs about
sweetly, the grandmother does shout
in reality their home has gone, sadly knocked down,
re-housed they were in another part of town
If you stay with me longer
then please excuse,
as my emotions get stronger and stronger,
work places that's no longer there
for I care to imagine the old Wolverhampton town
I shall go a wandering soon
in the early sun or
relax and observe the late moon
Why does sky on a Codsall evening
somehow ease my stress
and I'm powerless to
ride on a past time spree
around the Rough Hills or Fife
where my life is free
Aye, shall be going soon
in the first glimpse of sun
inspired by observing a
Staffordshire late night moon
Then I shall have to wait
to walk through the old swing gate

A Wulfrunian Way

into the daylight in my story
Time to tell of a recurring dream
realistic it does seem,
aah, I'm ten and then it was into my football field,
in the first part of my story
I've gone too far and thought too deep,
we were a band of brothers dreaming football in our sleep.
We didn't know it then but we knew when
time was time and now is the time for the football field
There's a hundred thousand and more
better poets than me,
but they don't tell my story
a word of my story

TREAT YOURSELF AULD LAD; to the February sunshine; It was a gathering of green space in gorgeous February sunshine. My first call was the West Park where I walked the perimeter and into the heart. It was noticeable that there were also others who wanted to take advantage of this lovely day. Credit must be given to everyone past and present who has contributed positively to Wolverhampton citizens. The 'feel good factor' is often needed and park space and well tended bedding can give you just that. The spaciousness was much appreciated and the wild life was in abundance. What a sight it was to witness the landing of a large white swan in the lake; such a show-off!

Next it was to the other side of town to walk the perimeter of the East Park. After completing I became a boy again; looking on over to where the pool and park was. A lad was peddling around in a some kind of cart as the pool was empty of water.

From there it was the shorter perimeter walk around Dixon Street playing fields and then Rooker Avenue. A hundred memories came to mind but it was obvious that both fields were missing children for whatever the reason;

not like our day. A midday bite to eat with my mother and off once more thinking "where shall I go to next?

The cemetery at Merridale was peaceful which gave me time to think while saying hello to my Owen kin. Soon I was parking up at Bantock Park which appeared to be quite busy with parents, children, grown-ups out for general exercise and dog- walkers. I was impressed with the path that's been laid almost all the way around. Snowdrops were in their hundreds and thousands making me want to be more green fingered.

I had done some miles, gone back a few years in thought and looked forward to my next trip to Scotland to do some more coastal walking. It felt good to be in that mindset.

I finished off with a well earned cup of tea at the cafe. Again I took advantage of the sunshine and sat alone at a table in the yard. "I don't do enough of this" I thought, because of my busy lifestyle. Not at any time was I more than a couple of miles from the city centre. I poured myself a cup of tea and to be honest it was that nice there I could've been anywhere in the British Isles.

Sarah Ann Darby and Joseph Williams

JOSEPH WILLIAMS A BLACKSMITH
FROM STEVENS GATE; 'How the mind plays with
Wolverhampton's bygone days.'
An early morning drive to get a photograph of a street where my great grandparents on the Williams side of the family lived. It is marvellous really how the desire to get to know more is suddenly fuelled. The previous day I had been studying a census, checking maps, finding the exact location and made my early morning plan to get there before it becomes busy. Having lived in Wolverhampton all my life I set off to find the street that I had passed by many times without knowing of my family history there.

    I park the car just a few yards down Pountney Street; there's one person walking up the street that I want to take the photograph of. He glances over at me as all I can do is kill a few seconds and fidget about with my mobile phone.

    Stevens Gate is as empty as it could be and the scene is set for me to take my photograph. There's no houses now just a man on Pountney Street with a mind full of imagination there in his ancestral gaze. So strong that he can see Joseph Williams, a blacksmith, aged 28 in 1901, returning home from a long day at work. Sarah Ann, his wife of two years younger, is in the street, with 4 month old Ellen (Nell) in her arms, waiting for him. By her side is her oldest daughter, also named Sarah Ann aged 4, and Ethel aged 2.

Joseph Williams, a Blacksmith from Stevens Gate ©

Robbie Kennedy Bennett

(28) **Joseph Williams, a Blacksmith from Stevens Gate** ©

Joseph Williams was a blacksmith
he married Sarah Ann Darby in All Saints,
and lived in Stevens Gate
in Wolverhampton's bygone days.
Looking up the census of 1901
all dwellings have gone from Stevens Gate,
now there's factories either side
I tried to picture Stevens Gate
in Wolverhampton's bygone days.
Joseph Williams was a blacksmith
wife and three daughters in Stevens Gate,
were there houses either side?
I visualised Stevens Gate
in Wolverhampton's bygone days.
Sarah Ann and the girls outside
playing in the street in Stevens Gate,
there in my ancestral gaze
drawn into Wolverhampton's bygone days.
All about Graisley and Dudley Road
there's a load knocked down and gone
since that census of 1901.
I stand on Pountney Street
a real short distance to Pearson Street
is Stevens Gate, little old Stevens Gate.
Where did that blacksmith ply his trade?
I wish I had something that he made
by hand, hammer, anvil and tongs,
when he lived on Stevens Gate.
Stevens Gate, why am I here?
this modern day, wanting yesteryear,
early morning, chosen for peacefulness;

A Wulfrunian Way

maximising all of late
when there's no place to indicate
a certain dwelling on Stevens Gate.
Joseph Williams the blacksmith
you I reinstate age twenty eight on Stevens Gate,
although impossible for us to meet
near to Lower Villiers Street and Bell Place
your way to work this man does trace;
how the mind plays
with Wolverhampton's bygone days.
"Stevens Gate, more than a quiet street
is Stevens Gate."

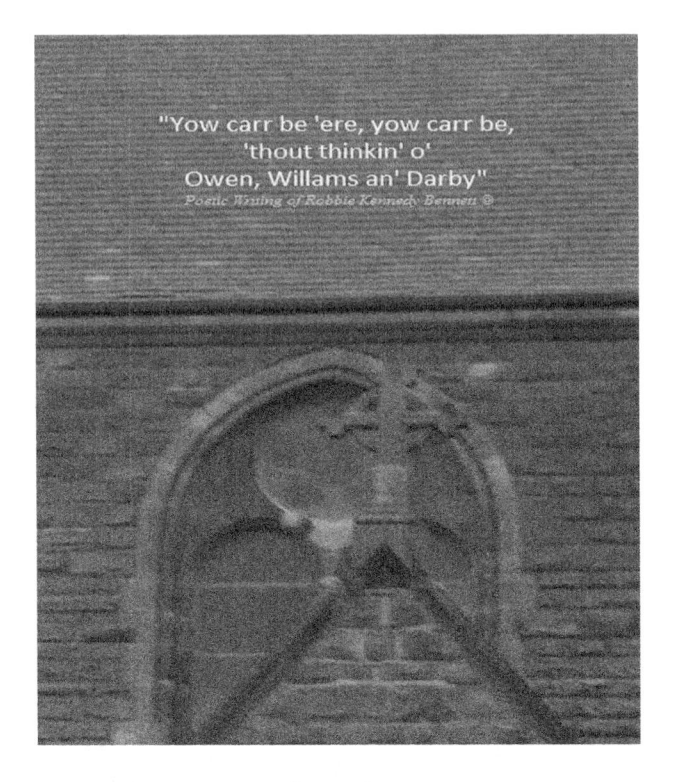

> "Yow carr be 'ere, yow carr be,
> 'thout thinkin' o'
> Owen, Willams an' Darby"
> *Poetic Writing of Robbie Kennedy Bennett ©*

OWEN, WILLIAMS AN' DARBY;

On a cold and windy Saturday morning in December 2018, two grandsons of mine are being asked to stand in a particular spot to have their photograph taken. They must be used to requests of mine such as this to do so as they were soon to be in position. These two boys were here to play football and I wanted a view of my school and church in the background. Another couple of footballers on the Owen, Williams and Darby bloodline with a link to All Saints, head for the playing area for their warm-up, which they certainly needed as it was bitter cold.

All Saints Church is now also used as a community

centre and the previous day my mother at the grand age of 89 had a Christmas lunch there. She thought the same thoughts that I have now; the wedding of Joseph Williams and Sarah Ann Darby in All Saints Church on Christmas Eve 1893.

"Do you Joseph Williams take Sarah Ann Darby?"
imaginable me, Christmas Eve of eighteen ninety three:
"for better, for worse, for richer, for poorer,
in sickness and in health"
fascinating, as all the way to now, I hear the vow,
as Joseph and Sarah Ann they both repeat some more
"according to God's holy law"

My mother was born a hundred yards from where I stand; her mother, Sarah Ann Williams died there a few weeks later. A couple of years afterwards Sarah Ann Darby also spent her last day there. A good reason for me to feel emotionally attached. Still within a hundred yards is the playground of my All Saints School childhood. The school in what was the start of my football journey in 1963. Perhaps that journey was already in progress and I was jumping on the train of life with carriages containing Owens, Williams, and Darby's.

Whenever there, this small area in Wolverhampton talks to me; what I hear and been taught is passed down. Those two lads setting off for training will know that there is a connection to here but exactly what, is for another time. They understand that it is me and gt nan Dot. I can't be here, I can't be; without thinking of my Wolverhampton roots. I look at the church and hear the voices of Joseph Williams and Sarah Ann Darby that say every vow. I shall never stop listening; no not ever in my lifetime.

(29) **Owen, Williams an' Darby** ©

Yow carr be 'ere, yow carr be,
'thout thinkin' o'
Owen, Willams an' Darby.
Win th' Gran' National,
Cheltenham Gold Cup an' th' Epsom Derby,
be rich an' famous but
yower conscience is stable an' hardy.
So yow carr be 'ere, yow carr be,
'thout thinkin' o'
Owen, Willams an' Darby.

JOSEPH WILLIAMS, SARAH ANN DARBY, I HEAR THE VOICES THAT SAY EVERY VOW; My Gt. Gt. Grandparents on the Williams and Darby line were married in All Saints on Christmas Eve 1893. Sarah Ann Darby, born in Eastwood Road, Rotherham. This could have been because of her father Sampson Darby working there. Joseph Williams at one time lived in Gower Street.

(30) **Joseph Williams, Sarah Ann Darby, I Hear the Voices That Say Every Vow** ©

Can't help looking and seeing family history,
not was it known by me then
when all that education pressure
was falling like showers;
hours and hours of being taught
now years after I am caught

very slowly, not swiftly
Church of All Saints and family history.
"Do you Joseph Williams take Sarah Ann Darby?"
imaginable me, Christmas Eve of eighteen ninety three:
"for better, for worse, for richer, for poorer,
in sickness and in health"
fascinating, as all the way to now, I hear the vow,
as Joseph and Sarah Ann they both repeat some more
"according to God's holy law"
Accordingly, the bride was born in Rotherham
to parents from here; meaning Wolverhampton;
I see Cheshire in the earlier generation
relation after relation a line it paints
a family line that takes me to All Saints.
Where I can't help looking and seeing family history,
life can be in some way a mystery,
that we have to solve, dig or explore;
perhaps it's all there in a room
and all you need is to open the door;
turn the handle as I did, very slowly, not swiftly
Church of All Saints and family history.
Fascinating, as all the way to now,
I hear the voices that say every vow.

AN OWEN KEPT GOAL FOR CHILLINGTON TOOL;

Two football team photographs, season 1925-26, appear to have been from a magazine called The Crocodile. I believe that it is from The Chillington Tool Company and may have been distributed to employees. Emblazoned across the chest of the shirt is a crocodile. The Crocodile is their trademark, first registered in England in 1876. With his roll neck jumper is a goalkeeper named J. Owen. This is Benjamin James Owen, mom's real dad. Many times as an Eastfield pupil I have passed by the works entrance without knowing of any family connection whatsoever. This one day in 2019 when walking about this area, I stopped to let my imagination take over. Later I was studying an aerial photograph of the works taken in 1928. In the background of a photograph of mine, unless mistaken, those buildings appear to be being built.

       I had an idea where their sports ground was in the 1960's, never played there myself, so to be sure I sent a message to Alan Alcock who replied,

"hi robbie,,,chillingtons pitch was at the rear of the factory behind the club,,if you stood outside east park gates the pitch was more or less in front of you,,,nothing left of it now all factory units,,,,as kids we would stand by the chain-link fence watching and hoping that one day that might be us out there,,,the players then looked ancient to us,but most were mid 30's,they had hard life working at the chillo,,,i wonder if billy howe has any info on them,,,,,anyway must go got to dubbin me boots lol,,,,,,take care and good luck with book,,,,"

(31) **An Owen Kept Goal for Chillington Tool** ©

James Owen kept goal for Chillington Tool
in the important canal and railway days,
arresting for it's interesting to see
team photos, contesting old team photos.
James Owen kept goal for Chillington Tool
a woollen rolled-neck jersey
manufacturing advertising style
every man in the picture looks prepared to play
displaying the Chillington brand of crocodile,
the well-known Chillington Crocodile.
James Owen kept goal for Chillington Tool
also an uncle told, Merthyr Tydfil.

A Wulfrunian Way

Old team photos at the moment are priority
a window to the past for
the evocative football-minded majority;
studious, such as I,
preoccupied, with seasons gone by.
Games I'd say on a Saturday afternoon
for men in the workplace
I should imagine couldn't come too soon,
around the green space of Wolverhampton.
Behind patriotism let's not hide
and the keeping of national pride,
recovering from wartime,
appreciative men to be in fresh air and outside,
joyous blokes, telling jokes, acting the fool,
after toiling at places such as Chillington Tool.
James Owen kept goal for Chillington Tool
also an uncle told, Merthyr Tydfil.
Eyes fixed, prepared for playing 'tween the sticks
in the season of 1925-26,
serious, not a smile in his jersey and crocodile
the well-known Chillington Crocodile.
James Owen dives, catches and slides
this ode is nothing more beside
my imaginative action replay ways
into the so called olden days.
Messrs. Barker, Foster and Jones
embedded in the Chillington history,
local industry and whoever knows,
social activity finds me, overflows,
arresting for it's interesting to see
team photos, contesting old team photos.
James Owen dives, catches and slides
bravely keeping his goal,
he crawls and slithers like a crocodile,
like the well-known Chillington Crocodile.

A Wulfrunian Way

Picture of Jim Owen and Nell Evans wedding

OWENS OF ALL SAINTS; An interesting Owen ancestry meeting happened at our house in Codsall. I had known Steve Owen through football for about 7 years. His lad played so I would often see Steve on the sideline at games. During one particular conversation of ours I asked the question that I often do. "Where does your Owen come from?" I was flabbergasted when he answered, "All Saints." I soon bombarded Steve with genealogy questions which he didn't know but he would ask his sister Tracy as she knows better. That meeting was on a Sunday afternoon and I made sure mom was in attendance. It came as no surprise that there was a definite link. Our Benjamin Owen born 1837 and baptised at St Leonard's, Bilston had a brother named Daniel, born 1823. Their father was Benjamin Owen born in Hanley Green and mother Sarah Whitehouse in Bilston. Tracy and Steve descend from Daniel Owen. As with my own offspring, I take pleasure knowing that those that I am related to play sport. In fact this season, 2019-20, a grandson of my cousin Jayne and myself are both playing for the same team.

Playing in football matches with or against relations at any level is always special. I may be mistaken but I believe that I have only done so twice. The first time was when I was with Sedgley Rovers and the opposition was Northicote Old Boys. Playing up front for them was Peter Darby, one of the spectators was Uncle Ben Owen. Afterwards Peter asked him what he was there for? He was surprised when finding out that in the opposing side was our Robbie, Dot's son! Another time was when I was playing in a cup game for Bilston Town against Brereton. I was in the away team and in the home side was 'Joey' Owen.

A promising footballer in the family was Joey Owen, son of Jim and Nell. He played in the 1970-71 FA Challenge Trophy at Wembley. This is a competition for clubs who pay their players therefore not eligible to play in the FA Amateur

Cup. There is a photograph on the Internet, by David Bagnall, of Joey, second player in line, following Telford United's manager, and former Wolves captain Ron Flowers onto the hallowed turf. Telford were winners that day beating Hillingdon Borough 3-2. Joey was to stay in the game after his playing days by managing a few non-league clubs. One being Bilston Town FC along with brother Alan as chairman.

Speaking to my uncles in the past, it appears that a few more in the family descending from Benjamin James Owen played the game of football. Fred Owen, who you shall read of later, told me in 2019 that Eddy was a decent amateur league player. I do know for a fact that he had grandsons who were good footballers. Also Emily Owen, his grandaughter is a professional having recently returned to West Bromwich Albion Women from Derby County having previously played for Aston Villa, Sheffield FC and Stoke City.

This one day in the Wolves Academy office, Nick Loftus, Education and Welfare Officer and long standing secretary of Wolverhampton Schools Football, brought in a shield that immediately got my attention. All Saints were winners in 1922-23 and again in 1923-24. I do not know if I had any relations playing in those games but would sure like to see the team line-ups.

(32) **Owens of All Saints** ©

Owens of All Saints
Kicked a casey
(Name for an old fashioned ball)
In the playground
Against the school wall
The streets of All Saints
And Steelhouse Lane
Eagle Street
Whence the Owens came
Owens of All Saints
Played their sport
Punched and kicked it
Batted and caught

In their uniforms
And in their teams
Owens held their own
It's in their genes
Owens of All Saints
In forces for wars of this world
Looking smart in their uniform
Man and girl
And upon a pitch
There is a descendant of
An Owen of All Saints
Me, a poetic artist
What a picture it paints!

OWENS MEET IN ST ANDREWS;
Part extracts of **WULFRUNIAN FOOTPRINTS IN FIFE** (2013);
My plan was to set out from my Codsall home as early as possible so I could get a day's walking in before going to the evening game (East Fife v Wolves, pre-season friendly 2013). Next day was also to be an early start to set off back to home as unfortunately my uncle Eddy Owen had passed away aged 89 and his funeral was early Thursday afternoon. He had also been a footballing man and whenever we were to meet he would call "get the ball out!

'In thought I cross the family divide' is a line in my poem 'Sojourn in St Andrews.' It is about my guilty feeling over a decade ago when in St Andrews. Here was I, a Wulfrunian boy realising and accepting I had a past somewhere other than Wolverhampton. I had always thought that at sometime a Scottish relation may step forward. 'Will I shake another by hand' is another line from my poem. Well I did so, at the gate of the Cathedral Ruins on Sunday afternoon. His name is Paul Owen, a direct cousin who has been a caddie on the Old Course for 20 years. Here is a surprise though, he's from Wolverhampton. We were waiting to meet Paul and I instantly knew it was him from over 100 yards away as he walked along the path in the ruins. It could have been a family instinct because of his stride and profile.

It was an enjoyable, emotional afternoon and evening with Paul and his partner Jacqui (now married) as we got to know each other. It was last summer that I was told by Joey and Alan (at Uncle Eddy's funeral), that Paul, their brother, lived in St Andrews. Neither one of us knew of each others link to St Andrews and accordingly I was told later by Paul that he had been talking of me ever since. This meeting made the trip worthwhile.

With cousin Paul Owen, St Andrews 2014

Some facts from Eddy Owen's eulogy below;
'In the army he was well into sport becoming a boxing and athletics champion. At the end of the war he was mentioned in dispatches for his bravery and also honoured by the Royal Humane Society. Afterwards Eddy was successful in his business career and in the 1980s acted as Chairman of the British Forging Industry Training Group. He was artistic and loved the outdoor life of caravanning and weekends away.'

I can recall Uncle Eddy being artistic as we had some paintings of his in our house. Also not long after we had moved to Codsall he hired the back room at the Crown as he was selling paintings by other artists. Reading about his love of the 'outdoor life of caravanning and weekends away' reminds me that we visited their caravan at Bridgnorth on a weekend. There's photographs of us in the 1950s, probably taken by Uncle Ben.

Uncle Eddy and Aunt Dot for a time had a caravan at Dinas Mawddwy, a small Village in the Snowdonia National Park. Uncle Jim and Aunt Nell used to go there with them sometimes. I think that I may have been once or twice with my family, but they definitely went more times after I was married. They stayed in a house in the village that was also the bank. Apparently people came from near and far to the pub which had an organ. Folk would gather around singing, Uncle Jim included, and it sounded wonderful.

A Wulfrunian Way

A Wulfrunian Way

ALWAYS AT MOLINEUX; July 13th 2020, listening to Mick McCarthy on GMB talking about the sad passing of Jack Charlton and how he treated people. Mick himself is very much the same. I can recall how he noticed me in arrivals at East Midlands airport and he immediately came over to join me. From then on he always waved when seeing me on the car-park at Compton Training Ground. A conversation in Molineux just after I had been awarded my 10 year service, and surprisingly his video message on my retirement after 21 years at Wolves; not forgetting to say "hello" for him to my cousin Paul Owen and his wife Jacqui in St Andrews next time I go up there! The likes of Jack & Mick would fit in any walk of life. It was after meeting up with Paul in St Andrews that I found out that he also knew Mick, most probably through golf.

I believe that it was mainly my Uncle Ben Owen and our Ricky (mom's cousin Eric Hodgetts) that I learned most from about Wolves of the 1950s and earlier. But then again, there was also my Grandad George Rowley who 'quietly' fed me information of the players before my time. It doesn't stop there - how can I forget when mom's other Owen brothers came visiting? All that football talk that filled the living room was bound to have an effect on this football daft youngster. The conversations were fantastic to listen to and be involved in, but it did make me wonder if I had been born too late? They all spoke highly of Stan Cullis, Billy Wright and more, so much that I felt that I knew them myself and that I had to go and see them one day. I see those statues now, Stan Cullis with his hat and Billy Wright with a football, and those relations of mine come to mind. Ricky Hodgetts and I even attended some Premier League games together which was nice for the both of us. An away game with Uncle Ben Owen is in the opening pages of my book 'Ode' Gold Wolves;

It was a painful early start of my support for the club when about 12 years of age. I had gone with my Uncle Ben to the away game and local derby against West Bromwich Albion at the Hawthorns. On returning to the railway station and boarding a packed football special, my hand was near to the hinge of the train door, within seconds the door was slammed shut from the outside with my little finger of my left-hand in the hinge. Needless to say it was a painful experience which resulted in a hospital visit and my finger in plaster for the next few weeks.

To be at Molineux is always special and social occasions are held there since the stadium was rebuilt. My mother wanted to celebrate her 80th birthday meal in Sir Jack's Restaurant and pictured is Stuart, my younger brother in Billy's Boot Room. Billy being legend Billy Wright, former Wolves and England Captain. Nine years later she chose the Molineux again and this time it was a party in the Hayward Suite.

A Wulfrunian Way

(33) **Always at Molineux** ©

Them old relations who fascinated me,
who very easily had this laddie's listening ear
by telling stories about games they'd been to
and players they'd seen.
The leaving of home for Molineux
Wolverhampton Coat of Arms
Bill Slater and the FA Cup at Wembley,
you painted football related pictures
that 60years later seem real;
the feeling of being there with you
is personal, somewhat personal.
Your support and vivid description
is carried to this day
progressively driving collectively on
gathering the young ones, the next ones.
They could've been tempted to scatter,
forget what's theirs and wear colours of another
but not to be, great to see,
the young ones, following suit, the next ones.
The leaving of home for Molineux
Wolverhampton Coat of Arms
Bill Slater and the FA Cup at Wembley.
Those old relations who fascinated me,
Owen, Williams and Rowley,
individually I could name - you're all to blame,
and the ground that captures our heart
called Molineux;
Now, those stories,
the feeling of being there for you
at Wembley, and always at Molineux.

A Wulfrunian Way

A BADGE ON A BLAZER, A SHIRT AND TIE (from my book 'Ode' Gold Wolves); I once wrote in the poem of mine 'Inherent Wolverhampton' that I could not remember ever being inside St Peter's Church. In 2015 came what I consider my first visit there when I was invited to the funeral service of our former owner Sir Jack Hayward. His close friend, colleague and Wolves vice-president gave a heartfelt and amusing eulogy that day and I felt honoured to have heard it first-hand. Hundreds of supporters were outside and Queen Square was packed out in gold and black as they watched the service on a huge screen. There is a terrific picture that captures that event well with the iconic statue of Prince Albert, fondly known as 'Man on the Oss,' surrounded by fans and townsfolk with the screen in the background.

(34) **A Badge on a Blazer, a Shirt and Tie** ©

Down in Dunstall the boy he came
in the course of time he built his name,
there lived young Jack,
turnstiles he once got under
the boy's a Wanderer
He kept on coming back
he kept on coming back,
he's a Wanderer
the boy's a Wanderer
He watched his heroes playing
forever we'll be saying,
he's a Wanderer
the man's a Wanderer
Forgetting not his Wolverhampton start
the football club was close to his heart,

A Wulfrunian Way

Arise Sir Jack,
he's a Wanderer
the man's a Wanderer
He kept on coming back
he kept on coming back,
because he's a Wanderer
the man's a Wanderer
The club he loved he was later to buy
and in the Bahamas under a clear blue sky,
there lived Sir Jack
and he'd be back
He kept on coming back
he kept on coming back,
he's a Wanderer
the man's a Wanderer
He wrote off debts for reasons why
a badge on a blazer, a shirt and tie,
there came Sir Jack
he's coming back
He kept on coming back
he kept on coming back,
he's a Wanderer
the man's a Wanderer
Flags are flying today at half mast
sadly supporters are walking past,
they've lost a fellow Wanderer
a special Wanderer
He kept on coming back
Rest in Peace Sir Jack,
we could have gone under
God bless, loyal Wanderer
A badge on a blazer, a shirt and tie
… a Wanderer shall never die,
'he kept the gold flag flying high'

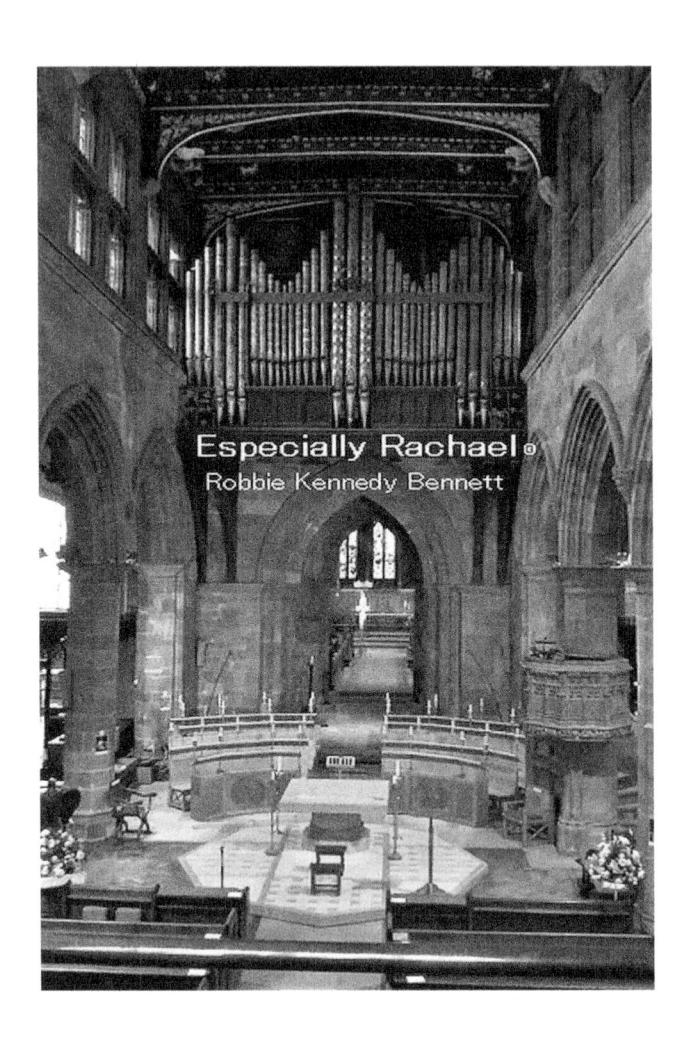

ESPECIALLY RACHAEL (from my book 'Ode' Gold Wolves); In February 2017 Rachael herself passed away after a short illness and once again I was there for the service in St Peter's Church. My invitation was high in the gallery and my early arrival gave me time to view and take in this magnificent church that is seen for miles. Soon I was to hear colleagues and sporting legends speaking fondly of Baroness Heyhoe Flint who was given freedom of the city in 2010. My own personal memory of Rachael is that she was a friendly and down to earth kind lady.

Later on making my way back to the ground to collect my car I found that I was following a couple of Wolves legends. Upon turning past the Molineux Hotel with that fantastic view of the stadium and out westward; I was within feet of Mike Bailey and Terry Wharton. Suddenly I was transported back to their playing days and my favourite entrance into the South Bank at Molineux. My poem 'Especially Rachael' brought lovely comments for this Wulfrunian who captained England and as said in a tribute became the "first global superstar of the women's game".

(35) **Especially Rachael** ©

Plenty of thoughtful time
and soon the occasion brought to mind
that 'we are Wolves,'
we are unique, 'we are Wolves,'
The infamous, the not,
black and gold in their heart they've got;
time of appreciation
if or not blood relation
draws a fellow to simply
respect who we are and what's earned
inside St Peter's Church, candles burned.
Rachael Heyhoe Flint
she deserved the praise,
hearts were lifted and raised,
oh, magnificently the choir sang,
around St Peter's their voices rang
for Rachael.

A Wulfrunian Way

Words, they hit every note,
humorously someone wrote,
of Rachael.
Two hours soon went by
I stepped out of St Peter's Church
my eyes up high in the Wolverhampton sky,
for Rachael;
within a minute or two our home of the Molineux
I was looking upon,
the likes of Rachael are never gone.
Those colours I saw on a supporters scarf
cannot be separated or cut in half,
like the eight day of the week;
we are unique, 'we are Wolves,'
especially Rachael.

(36) **My Bilston Road Beginning** ©

It was down by New Inns it was
where in modern days trams do pass,
I joined the working class I did
the proud old working class.
Schooldays all done
this lad to become a wage earner
a novice, a learner,
classrooms are on the back burner!
It was down by New Inns I went
where in modern days trams do pass,
I joined the wage earning working class
and noticed me you may
possibly, on my first working day?
A painter, decorator, builder's mate
of some sort, was the plan;
given the job by a man
who rode a motorcycle and sidecar.

A Wulfrunian Way

Looking out for me;
"Be there on the Bilston Road,
by the Steelway, young lad,"
first job I had it was
the very first job I had,
you could have seen me, waiting?
Off to Frost and Sons at Moxley,
approximately a fifteen minute ride,
he didn't go fast,
unfortunately my first job
didn't last long, in fact
six weeks to be exact.
Recently you may have seen me
as I drove through Coven to Brewood?
yes two days back I did,
and I can't get rid of the time
to a house where I was working
I rode that bike of mine;
what year was it? blimey - 1969!
Age fifteen, you should've seen me
leave Rough Hills, out of town
down Stafford Road,
beads of sweat on my brow
tell you now, how could I forget,
it's clear as glass
my introduction to the working class.
Then, on that bike from Rough Hills to Penn
struggled at times when,
recall it still, pushing my bike
o'er Goldthorn Hill,
phew! You could've helped me!
My second job, it didn't last long as well
but houses I can still tell you where,
yes tell you where as occasionally I pass
early days of mine in the wage earning working class.

A Wulfrunian Way

Longer service and loyalty followed on
years flew by, time has gone quick,
I flick through the pages of living
in the well read book of life,
perhaps you lived it with me?
Retirement does loom
I never come out of that room
of knowing where time has taken
since my Bilston Road beginning.
The simplicity of certain place names
bus stops, buildings and me
no where near a mass,
not being over confident or bold as brass,
profession - the crystal clear clarity of progression
when first, I joined the wage earning working class.
Yesterday - as a stranger, once a teenager,
watched as vehicles pass,
where I joined the working class.
As a matter of not being important,
you may have forgotten me?

WHEN ARE YOU GOING TO FIND TIME?;

An olde worlde feel down by the canal bridges at New Cross and a good starting point for a much needed long walk. It's now been 5 months since my spinal surgery and 3 weeks into retirement, so I was due to make some time to test myself. There was a welcome sight of wildlife so close to human activity. Ducks dived noisily into the canal on the housing side because of being disturbed by the presence of a cat. A cluster of wild poppies as always made me think of those who gave all. Just then near to Swan Garden Bridge and as I was feeling glad to be somewhere different, two lilac thistles made me think of when I can pick-up my walking in Scotland. It all started in 2007 when walking the Fife Coastal Path in stages. In total now I can look at a map and see that I went beyond that, having walked from Dalmeny on the south side of the Firth of Forth, around Fife and over the Tay into Angus. Arbroath is where I have got to now and the clock of life is ticking so I best get thinking about it. Passengers looked inquisitively down on me, or perhaps out of boredom from a stationary cross country train on the railway bridge near Horsley Fields Junction. It soon got moving after having clearance to approach the train station. "The next train to arrive at platform one" I heard just as I did last night after travelling back home to Codsall after having a drink with my brothers in the Great Western. Industrial history was jumping out at me to see. I crossed Broad Street at Wolverhampton Top Lock and the canal scenery changed. Water gushed out of lock number 3 making me watch for a short while. Lock number 5 at Cannock Rd, drivers were stationary in traffic in their motor-vehicle world and I was pressing on in the water-world of mine. "When are you going to find time" I said to myself meaning to get back up to Arbroath? Lock 16 by Dunstall Viaducts and scenery changed once again as number 17 out of town took me out into Aldersley and Pendeford with the sound of town decreasing until hardly anything. I got off at Bilbrook and followed the footpath sign. My shadow on the recently cut grass seemed to be doing better than I was as I made my way across the fields. If you find time lad you'll need to get some practice in! Once I get to the high school it's only a mile from home and a welcome hot bath.

(37) **When Are You Going to Find Time** ©
When are ye gonna find time Rab?
tae come uptae Arbroath,
tae pick up yer coastal walk Rab
where the smokies smoke.
Where the herring smoke lad
good tae see ye on that coast lad,
sae come uptae Arbroath Rab
where the smokies smoke.

EAST PARK HAPPINESS; It was mid-morning when I arrived at the East Park to spend a nostalgic hour or so connecting with my childhood. The time went quickly and soon it was 11.00am. Truth of the matter is that I had walked the perimeter of the park quicker than I thought that I could. Was the park bigger in my childhood day or did it just appear so?

      The embankments, shape of the side walk, heat from the concrete, imagining it on my bare feet; under the midday sun, it was as hot and bright as I remember.

A Wulfrunian Way

(38) **East Park Happiness** ©

Clock strikes eleven
as if beckoning me to look, come near,
welcoming - think away - there's nothing to fear
sincerity in silence, after strikes of eleven
be eleven boy, be eleven.
Pools empty, park I played on is gone,
golf, no more - it wasn't when I was eleven.
Over yonder - eight Union Flags fly,
East Park Wolves, Cycle Speedway Club
I pause out of interest
as this was new to me when walking on by.
A childhood call, I crave for youth
where my nineteen-sixties were spent
aye I miss you so much,
here where my walking boots touch.
Hark! I can hear my laughter
sense my joy, in the July sunshine
becoming that boy again,
but all that's no more, still feels a shame.
I walk the paths in remembrance
have I ever stepped down there
have I ever climbed, in East Park happiness
in those young days of mine?
East Park happiness then noon it did chime
returning me to - elderly living -present time...
sincerity in silence I delve
as I fight to become twelve.

THE GROOVES IN THE OLD CORNER BRICK; My first call on this Friday morning walk was at Holy Trinity Church at Heath Town. This so because family history of Wheaton and Darby found to be there; since then there feels a connection. Weather looked a little bit mixed but I was patient enough to wait for the sun to break through and shine on the church spire. I entered the canal at Deans Road Bridge and headed for Horseley Fields Junction. It was a left-turn from there that was my point of interest today as I wanted to revisit my canal world of bygone time. On the brickwork of the bridges were the grooves from the ropes of the horses that pulled the barges. I wrote a poem of this back in 2004. The industrial feelings of my younger years were surfacing more by the second. I passed by BOC and still reminded that my relation Ricky once worked there. What is strange is that I have always thought that, even as a teenager when passing by as a schoolboy from Eastfield. Bilston Road Bridge was soon upon me as signs of the modern day stores that I am familiar with came into view. A tram went by on its journey towards Bilston and beyond. At the time I was deep in thought as to where Benjamin Owen (gg grandfather) lived as his address on the 1861 Census is Canal Side when age 24. He was to stay in this area as he later lived the back of Eagle Works employed at Edge Tool. He died age 49 at an address on Bilston Road. I took my time thinking of life in those days and how tough it was. Beyond Bilston Road Bridge and into my own past. As a youth I worked at Delta and as I turned the bend the casting area came into view near to Cable Street Bridge. I took a photo and a cyclist stopped and asked if it was of wild flowers? We engaged in conversation and I explained that there was a tall building here called the B4 press back in my day. Just afterwards a barge named Hobgolin with a Welsh flag passed me by as a friendly wave of a hand came my way. I searched for a door that was opened by the B5 press to allow heat out and fresh air in. I can remember the occasional few seconds or so taken to look out on the canal and over to GKN, formerly BJB which is being built on and soon to become housing. I reached my destination for canal walking at Dixon Street Bridge which was nearest to my childhood home. I can recall the bridge being built and how I had to carry my bicycle over a footbridge. The shape and bend of this part of the canal pulled me back in time, red poppies welcomed and reminded me of those that gave their all for our freedom. I can remember realising that I could cycle alongside the canal from here quite easily to Aunt Shirl and Uncle Bill's house in Crown Street. I came up with the idea that I could make a trailer to take Stuart with me. He'd be about six years old: It never got as far, never mind beyond the design board.

A cup of tea at mom's and then off towards town along Steelhouse Lane and Cleveland Road. Going up Dudley Street just blending in when a strong hand of a fellow in a Wolves polo shook mine. Within a short while I was walking through St Peter's Gardens towards the station thinking I would probably have to wait for a train. "Yours is just pulling into Platform 1 now" said the friendly girl in the ticket office. Ten minutes later I stepped off the train at Codsall and back into modern day after having the time of my life.

The canal was a major player for the Wolverhampton ancestors of mine. Transporting of goods was needed during The Industrial Revolution and because of the demands the canal system was built. Many a few hours of my growing up years was spent down on the towpath at Dixon Street bridge. Less than half a mile away there was an entrance to a world heaped in history. I was fascinated, and still am today of the grooves cut by rope on the corners of the brickwork. These were made by strong horses pulling the loaded barges back and forth of their destination. There was a few factories on our side of town, so my ancestors relied on the canal.

I miss living close to a canal where I can easily hop on and off. The nearest to my house is going out of Bilbrook towards the Stafford Road. The direction of the Shropshire Union Canal to Brewood is still rural, so it would have been towards Autherley Junction and Wolverhampton in the Victorian Era as the housing development was yet to be built. Without doubt there would've been much canal traffic navigating their way through the area. I follow a map of the canal along the Old Main Line, counting down those locks to Broad Street. Names from censuses, birth and death registers, work history, jump out at me, proving that we needed to live somewhere near a canal. Horsley Fields, Walsall Street, Chillington Basin, Bilston Street, Monmore Green, then Dixon Street, from there I stepped off the towpath, I was a boy again, and I was home.

(39) **The Grooves in the Old Corner Brick** ©

There was no river for us to walk alongside
but a towpath by the cut our bikes we could ride,
and we cycled for hours and hours
we cut shelter under bridges in showers.
We studied the grooves in the old corner brick
they were cut from ropes an inch or more thick,
when horses pulled barges along the path side
was they bred to do this until the day that they died?
Was it cruel or did they have strength
how heavy are barges and what is their length?
And we'd watch the barge men operate the lock
on occasions they'd wave and pull over to dock.
The towpath was a lesson in time
when cargo was delivered by a barge on a line.
And we studied the grooves in the old corner brick
they were cut from ropes an inch or more thick,

A Wulfrunian Way

> I know that they're still there today
> 'though it's been many a year since I've been there to play,
> that age in time I imagined of course
> man relied on the old trusty horse.

(40) **Poppies by All Saints Church in July** ©

Poppies by All Saints Church
undoubtedly beautiful:
there, in a special place, growing wild;
then swiftly, quite suddenly,
I see through the eyes of a child
poppies by All Saints Church in July.
Hark!.... I hear a cry,
"War Declared Against Germany"
by Great Britain in August of 1914,
how topical, that news would've been.
Each and every one of you,
none of who I name,
'Poppies by All Saints Church'
respectful feelings duly came.

A Wulfrunian Way

The Wolvo Old Roads

Scottish
Wulfrunian
creating writing of RKB ©
since 1989

(41) **The Wolvo Old Roads** ©

The old roads - interesting old roads,
hold a lot of imagination.
Ran, cycled, drove or walked along,
the old roads - the Wolvo old roads.
Sing a song about the old roads;
make it up as I go along the old roads,
the old roads - the Wolvo old roads.
Memories jump out of the old roads
sunshine or raining,
all weather, marathon training,
refraining from being lazy
the crazy-man running all weather
down the old roads - the Wolvo old roads.
Revisit them now but at a different pace
walk them now and not a stressful race,
drive along, sometimes along the old roads.
The Ring Road
you interrupt the old roads,
plenty Wolvo old roads,
but when my eyes are closed
I see them - embedded in mind are the old roads.
Factories, houses and conveniences,
close to hand amenities,
schools that educated geniuses,
on the old roads - interesting old roads,
the Wolvo old roads that I wander.

OFTEN AT ALDERSLEY;
Back in the childhood day Hugh Porter's mother used to call at our house collecting the Rediffusion TV rental payments: his named road sign always reminds me of our mothers chatting friendly in our hall. In 1973 Hugh received his MBE for his services to cycle racing. The colours of the field and track were quite visible in some parts through the trees of the South Staffs Railway path. I was at Aldersley where the stadium has intertwined for much of my life. Back in the childhood day it was school athletics, where twice I became the Staffordshire Cross Country winner for Eastfield. In my young adult day it was football cup finals and representative games.

In the 1980s, before the demolition of the old building, it was the venue for some of the local road races, such as The Turkey Trot and Wolverhampton 10. There are a few old photos of my running days stored somewhere in our house. One includes Ken, that's Wendy's husband at the time, and myself walking across the old car park to the starting position.

Then came my mid-life day when the following 21 years representing Wolves Academy. Most recently it has been the venue for a grandson and his winter training, which I take him more often than not.

As much as I try, I can't remember the railway line. Less than a stone's throw from the roads that I drive regularly, the feeling of being in another world. Shaded by heavily leaved trees which will later this year thin in the season of Autumn.

Soon I'm under the sturdy bridge of the Tettenhall Road and Cupcake Lane Tea Room is in view. This is a lovely old station and so nice to see that it still has a life. I turn around to have a second look and imagined a train pulling alongside the platform. Here in my elderly day at Compton Bridge, which appears to be busy as the noise level increases because of the traffic. I shall switch-off now, and get on the canal towpath and walk back to Aldersley; not before watching some folk navigate the mechanism at Compton Lock.

FAIRIES FIELD; There was a reader of the Black Country Bugle that asked the question about how a specific field in Blakenhall got its name. "Fairies Field" or "Fairy's Field" was south of Caledonia Road and east of Pond Lane. One of mom's earliest memories is being pushed very quickly in a pushchair by her mother (Jane/Gin Rowley). The reason being is that they were being chased by a horse! They got behind a gate of one of the houses just in time. She thinks that it may have been a horse of Wally Hales which opened up another story. Ken Owen was riding a horse and cart of Wally's. He was young and so small at the time and although he held the reigns he could not be seen.

Not the best quality photograph of three Owen brothers and their wives. Ken and Sybil; Eddy and Dot; Jim and Nell, but great to see them together.

A Wulfrunian Way

HERE'S TO KNOWING MORE OF MR OWEN; Cars of mine have been parked in places of Wolverhampton and more than I can mention in Scotland, all in the interest of family history. Today I was joined by Richard Fardoe, another in the Owen and Williams lines that we share. We were at Jeffcock Road, Merridale and then Holy Trinity Church, Heath Town. An informative two hours for the both of us and to be honest it was well overdue. We both agree that times were obviously tough for our ancestors as they travelled far finding work. Mostly our family were born locally to Wolverhampton but Sarah Anne Darby in Rotherham and her maternal grandfather Isaac Wheaton in Budworth estimated 1809 are in our tree. It was good to be joined on this venture with someone having the same genealogy interest. We both set our sights on finding the next Owen generation beyond Benjamin born 1801 in Hanley Green in the Potteries. Marvellous really as it's only in recent years that I have known of Merridale and Heath Town, which for me was only where the swimming baths was that I attended. The name of the church next door being Holy Trinity would have been a question that I would've got wrong in a quiz about Wolverhampton.

(42) **Here's to More Knowing of Mr Owen** ©

I know he was born in Hanley Green
and wed Sarah in Sedgley,
here's to more knowing of Mr Owen and his kin
during Georgian and pre-Victorian times;
then for him came the coal mines,
the Staffordshire coal mines.
Winters were long - he had to be mentally strong,
Mr Benjamin Owen - to keep going,
here's to more knowing of Mr Owen and his kin

to put food in a bowl - he started mining the coal;
hard times, and the Staffordshire Coal mines.

(43) **The Distance to Town Seemed Longer When I Was a Kid** ©

The journey on the number 30 bus
seemed like forever
it went up Major Street,
I stand to be corrected, but I recall,
through the right-hand window
I saw the orange-bricked factory wall.
Back of the 'Monkey' on the other,
Kent Road and Bayliss's Sports Ground,
looking back now I try to remember all that I did,
the distance to town seemed longer when I was a kid.
The house on the right-corner
was grannie and grandad's, so mom said,
was it to be Caledonia Road Off Licence
or Adey's instead?
Soon I would need to choose,
not for booze but for treats and sweets,
big jars on shelves and big hands to screw-off the lid,
the distance to town seemed longer when I was a kid.
Reynolds lived one side Marandola the other,
two lads my age,
as the book of life started turning page by page,
All Saints Church and schools
I could never repay,
mom was barmaid in the Summerhouse,
back in that day.
Joey's jailhouse, terraced houses,
and shop after shop,
I wish I was on that bus

A Wulfrunian Way

near Gordon Street hopping off,
I'd turn around ten times
one hundred and eighty degrees,
Victorian houses and smoke
from chimneys, yes please.
Walk to The Royal Hospital, laugh,
staff knew me well,
many times it was needed
my medical records could tell,
the Bilston Road island sadly it isn't no more,
my vision of past-time doesn't leave
as there's no exit door.
Suddenly, there on Bilston Street what do I see?
the number 30 bus has stopped
and is waiting for me,
so I run without falling for the driver
and conductor are calling
sixty years later this laddie
said thanks and hopped on,
thinking where on earth
have those sixty years gone?
Dreams and memories like this I never can rid,
as the conductor he spoke
and showed me an old paper quid
"bet the distance to town seemed longer
when you was a kid."

SOME SORT OF WULFRUNIAN TRAIL; It's Friday morning in September 2019 that I arrived at All Saints to walk My Wulfrunian Trail. This was less of a journey from my Codsall home as much of my ancestral walking, because of my dad, has been on the coast of Scotland (search Wulfrunian Footprints in Fife). For a few days I had been listing addresses of mom's family and very soon my route was made.

A Wulfrunian Way

    I parked my car outside of the church which I was well familiar with as a schoolboy and where my grandparents Benjamin James Owen and Sarah Ann Williams married in 1915. Crossing over Steelhouse Lane by The Summerhouse pub and into Eagle Street, home of the Owen family. I paused for a minute to set my mind on those days in a street where much has changed, meaning having no housing.

> 'Isaiah Owen, your dad put his mark
> he couldn't write, but I bet he could work
> from morning to night, aye until dark,
> can't see him as a fool,
> Benjamin Owen, born in the Potteries
> a hoe maker at Edge Tool.'

At the bottom of Eagle Street was Eagle Works where Isaiah Owen spent his working days. Modern day trams run down Bilston Road these days and I had to cross over to get to Commercial Road where those of mine lived and Benjamin James Owen was born. The family would have witnessed close-up the change that was about to happen to Wolverhampton and surrounding area. One year after the arrival of Benjamin James Owen came the power station.
    The Commercial Road Power Station opened in 1895, built because of the 1888 Electric Lighting Act. It was powered by coal transported in on the nearby canal. The cooling tower landmark was to be captured on most pictures in a certain mile radius. It certainly did in photographs of All Saints pupils taken on the front playground in the 1950's and 60's. The cooling tower was demolished on a day of poor visibility in 1977.
    I walked along York, Duke, St James and Union

Streets where my Williams, Darby and Farnell families lived. Different housing but the very fact that at one time or other, they would have written or told someone of these addresses is significant in my story. Modern building and businesses are plenty but the older architectural construction attracted my attention such as Chubb & Sons Lock & Safe Company which was just visible from Corn Hill as I made my way down to Sun Street. This was the last dwelling of a great grandfather, Isaiah Owen.

(Picture of The Great Western, corner of Corn Hill and Sun Street. The dwellings have gone and is now the pub's car park. Isaiah Owen's last known address and where he died at number 4 New Sun St.)

I circled the street of the Great Western pub and started to make my way back up the hill but returned to take a photo. Admiration had surfaced because of the Low Level Station and I wished that it had been possible to keep this and other buildings and areas as a living museum. Wolverhampton has changed plenty in my time and full concentration is needed as I approach the ring-road to get to my next port of call.

> 'What I shall do Mary Farnell sweet Mary Farnell
> is visit the church of St John's, Wolverhampton,
> I will wait outside and see you come outside
> a young and happy, smiling beautiful bride,
> oh Mary Farnell sweet Mary Farnell.
> Also for Lucy, dearest Lucy,
> I will wait outside and see her come outside
> a young and happy, smiling beautiful bride,
> and Mary, sweet Mary, will you wait there with me?'

Into the modern era I go, negotiating the decision made of pedestrian planning on the Ring-Road; which was built in sections over a 26 year period commencing in 1960. Within a few minutes I was to notice in St John's the final resting place of Rev. Henry Hampton. St John's Church being next on my list; two sets of brides and grooms, plus guests, would think that it was unlikely that such a busy wide road would come so close to here a century or so later. That being so, the magnificent looking St Paul's Church at the junction of the Penn Road, built in 1835 and demolished in 1960's because of the Ring-Road expansion. Shame really as I so much wanted to see the newly wed Mr&Mrs Wardley exit the church doors in 1867. It proved to be difficult to leave a piece of open space without imagining the church and working out exactly where it was. Vehicles sped past me onto the A449 in a snake-like fashion heading for Penn and beyond. I was to follow but only the short distance to find

Graisley Hill.

> 'Oh St Paul's, you looked so prominent
> so dominant, so well designed,
> now, you are something I can't find,
> marriage, death and birth
> your structural being has left the earth.'

The imagination of St Paul's Church had given in to visualising housing on Graisley Row. Street signs, the actual shape of the roads and those known who walked along had to be acceptable for me. These days we find it too easy to get into a car and drive to places that we can walk to. If I recall correctly the Wolverhampton Marathon route in the 1980's that I ran was near: but there is too much focus in running; a planned walk these days is a great teaching and learning experience for me. The Wardley's house in Graisley Row and nearest church is locked in the past; nevertheless, I enter the year of 1901 and head for Steven's Gate.

> 'Joseph Williams was a blacksmith
> he married Sarah Ann Darby in All Saints,
> and lived in Stevens Gate
> in Wolverhampton's bygone days.
> Sarah Ann and the girls outside
> playing in the street in Stevens Gate,
> there in my ancestral gaze
> drawn into Wolverhampton's bygone days.'

Bell Place is a road that I was not too familiar with and although I may have been on it at sometime in my life, I would never have known the name, until I found that it is where the first home was of my Rowley nan and grandad. In my young days they lived in First Avenue, Low Hill and I can't help but associating them with that side of town. This walk of mine is in the footsteps of the earlier days of Rowley and Williams plus more. It's time now to leave the Graisley area and cross over the Dudley Road which no doubting was done many times by family of mine in past-time.

Travelling out of Wolverhampton would be on Green Lane which was to change to Birmingham Road. Thompson Avenue was previously a less significant road to Parkfield Road. The Birmingham New Road was opened by the Prince of Wales in 1927. Studying a map surveyed by Isaac Taylor and published in 1751, the roads out of this side of town were to Dudley, Bilston and Walsall. Unless I am mistaken my present position, which is out of picture, would be mostly open fields; a lane, or soon to be, leading to Cockshut and Rough Hills Collieries. The Crown in Cartwright Street, built about 1861 and still open today, perhaps had a certain Rowley (great grandfather), who was a holloware japanner neighbour as a customer around 1901.

On one particular Victorian map there is only Cartwright Street off Dudley Road and not beyond what is now the Birmingham Road. Other than a brick work, there is open land and All Saints Church and Schools would be visible. I gazed for a while and thought of former times. So realistic was the imaginative mind of mine as I considered walking down the quiet Green Lane (now Birmingham Road) to Rough Hills Colliery and introducing myself to a miner named Samuel Williams - this a great, great grandfather of mine.

On the road back now I maunder to All Saints Schools and Church, but before doing so I made a detour into The Square by Derry Street. The reason being is that I wanted to see a house still standing of my Rowley great grandparents. As a boy I had frequented this many times as dad worked in a scrapyard at the back - opposite the

Builders Arms on Derry Street. I longed for my grannie to wave at me from her front door.

All in all there was nothing really to discover, only the self-satisfaction that I have walked their roads and connected with their churches. What had struck me, was how close their homes were and how soon this walk was completed.

Same as walking over the Kinkell Braes into St Andrews in Fife, this time where another family home was in Gower Street into All Saints Road. There by the church are another set of ancestors who greet me with glee on their hard working faces. I felt rich with love. Thank you dear reader for 'tagging along' with me these last 180 years on some sort of a Wulfrunian trail.

KISS JANE CORBETT, THE BEAUTIFUL BRIDE;

Manufacturing history was soon to be in the making behind St Paul's Church with the development of 'Sunbeamland.' The Sunbeam Factory in Paul Street was a major place of employment for the town. The company started with the making of bicycles, then motorcycles and cars. After merging with a French company in 1920, they were the first British car to win a Grand Prix race and set land speed records. This I'm sure would've inspired the employees massively. Sadly from a great height came a low when in 1977 the Sunbeam Factory was abandoned. The Wolverhampton Civic Society recognised the contribution of Sunbeam with a blue plaque on the landmark building that is quite visible from the ring-road. Yours truly, stares at the ground in front where a religious building once was. Jane Corbett, born 1848, daughter of Maria, was the bride to be. I was too late to see the church and imagine my Gt x 4 Grandparents arrival.

(44) **Kiss Jane Corbett, The Beautiful Bride** ©

They married in St Paul's in 1867
James and Jane; April rain was it falling?
Perhaps be the weather was fair
James and Jane; I wish that I was there,

A Wulfrunian Way

impossible but I don't care:
I would disguise, unrecognisably I would hide,
to see the groom and bride.
James Wardley, Jane Corbett,
arriving at the church of St Paul,
should I shout, should I call?
James and Jane, I am here, 1867 was the year:
shame that I have to hide, as I'd love to kiss the bride.
Oh St Paul's, how I see you
on the ring road, by the Penn Road
the modern day ring road, oh St Paul's,
how I see you, on the ring road.
Oh St Paul's, you looked so prominent
so dominant, so well designed,
now, you are something I can't find,
marriage, death and birth
your structural being has left the earth.
St Paul's, you're more than hidden,
the suggestion of destruction should've been forbidden,
was the objection overridden?
Meaning I can't be outside as much as I've tried
filled up with pride, to kiss Jane, the beautiful bride.

ST PAUL'S CHURCH; There are some fantastic photographs of St Paul's Church, built about 1835 and surprises me that it was demolished in 1960. One image is with the ring road island and underpass in place, and only a few cars and lorries nearing the Penn Road. Nowadays it's a wider road with the church making way for traffic flow. Blakenhall flats are in the background and in the foreground is the Fox Hotel. St Paul's Church really does look a magnificent building, but try as I might I can't remember it being there. In one way it looks a relatively modern view because of the pedestrian underpass and direction of the roads. Another is a Victorian drawing of the church 1897-1900, looking prominent in quite a rural setting. One description I found is that it was a 'handsome structure of mixed architecture.' Yes I would definitely agree with that.

Afterwards I was to realise that James Wardley and Jane Corbett married at that church over 30 years earlier of that artistic image, showing a yet to be built road and footpaths. A gentleman in a top hat is in conversation with what looks like a lady in her riding gear on a horse. Walking past them, on what would be the Penn Road now, is a mother in a bonnet and daughter in a brim hat, both wearing long skirts. I can't make out who the artist of this drawing or possibly painting is, but I can see that it was for Rev W. Dalton and Robt Ebbels (Ebbles) Archt. The Reverend William Dalton, from Northern Ireland, mainly paid for the church. He became the first vicar of St Paul's (1835-59).

THE ROWLEY NAME; I was to grow up knowing that we had a link to the footballing Rowley brothers through grandad George Rowley. As I got older I wanted to know exactly how this football-daft lad was related to this famous duo. My poem 'The Rowley Name,' written in 2007, was printed on the Football Poets website. I also added into my first book Awa' th' Rough Hills an' Awa'.

Jack Rowley, (John Fredrick Rowley) at the time of writing is in 4th place in the all time record goal scoring for Manchester United. Wayne Rooney is first then Sir Bobby Charlton and Denis Law CBE. According to the 1939 census, John F., still unmarried, is a labourer at the local gas works. He lives with his parents, Mark, a brass moulder, and Hannah, at 83 Myatt Avenue in Wolverhampton, along with his two older sisters. He married Violet M. Ward [registered in Wolverhampton, March 1942]. His football career was interrupted because of the war and he served in the South Staffordshire regiment, participating in the D-Day landings.

Arthur Rowley, (George Arthur Rowley) scored a

record of 434 goals and was later player-manager at Shrewsbury Town. Apparently because of his 'explosive' left-foot, he was known as 'The Gunner.' For a time he had an astonishing goal-scoring rate (7-in 10 games) but surprisingly never got capped for England, although at the time of his death a national newspaper stated that 'no Englishman had a better eye for goal.' Not being selected could be because much of his career was in the lower divisions. After retirement he was manager at Sheffield United and Southend United.

My research is that grandad George Rowley's father, Thomas Albert Edward Rowley, is half-brother to Mark Rowley, a semi or pro- goalkeeper with Walsall, and the footballers dad. This is also the opinion of Richard, son of Sheila Fardoe nee Owen.

It has also been passed down in the family that grandad George Rowley trained the brothers when they were boys. With him being 14 & 20 years older and known to be a good footballer himself that could possibly be true. Something that caught my attention was that I found Arthur named as George 'Arthur' Rowley Jr on the internet. So could he have been named George Rowley Jr after grandad?

*Thomas Albert Edward Rowley b1874
with George Rowley b 1906*

(45) **The Rowley Name** ©

In my line is the Rowley name,
Goal scoring records and football fame.
War torn interrupted professional careers,
Once more I reflect on bygone years.
My Grandad was a Rowley too,
Been paid to play if he wanted to.
But Nan she always knew the score,
Keep the bad wolf from our door.
A cartilage injury I also heard,
Was that the reason and not Nan's strong word.
So cousin George chose not to play the game,
Jack and Arthur progressed to football fame.
When he was about age sixty-seven,
I would then be around eleven.
We were kicking a ball on a Somerset beach,
My modern skills I tried to teach.
But he had such a delicate touch,
That impressed I can't describe how much.
I forgot my Grandad was a Rowley too,
Been paid to play if he wanted to.
I noticed how soon he selected his pass,
On a Somerset beach not on a field of grass.
One day when I was just sixteen,
I played right back in a pro-Youth Team.
He came to Stafford to see me play,
I remember it well, except the score that day.
Come the time about twenty-two,
I knew it all like young men do.
He was watching me play there on the line,
I think that day I was number nine.
I can't recall another game,
After that match that my Grandad came.

A Wulfrunian Way

I've never forgot he was a Rowley too,
Been paid to play if he wanted to.
Although time fades and less they preach,
I saw it all on a Somerset beach.
Goal scoring records and football fame.
The highly reputable Rowley name.

Pictured is Granny Rowley (Mary) nee Bennett, with grandaughters, Shirley on her lap, Evelyn, Mary and Dorothy (front right). Albert Rowley and Mary Bennett lived in the Square near Vicarage Rd. Mary Bennett's parents were George Bennett and Mary Ann Risby, being my aunt Jan and Shirl's gt grandparents. Their gt,gt, grandfathers are James Bennett and Enoch Risby.

NOAH WILLIAMS; February 2020 and for a second time on social media I posted my poem 'Dr Wallace on Snow Hill.' Once again it got a very good response from not only my own but members of a certain Wolverhampton Facebook page. Dr Wallace had a small farm at Kingswood according to Paul Webber and his brother was the manager for a few years. Phillip Hodgetts, a family member, son of Mill and Ern, commented that Dr Wallace was a friend of Uncle Noah, a self-made man and both of them owned racehorses. Upon speaking to my mother about this, she knew of the horses but couldn't recall them being kept for racing. Mother and I were soon into talking about Uncle Noah and his hut that was on the Rough Hills playing field. She mentions that Marie (Marion) as a young girl was in the shop and called him Mr Williams. Uncle Noah replied jokingly, "What's the matter, am I not good enough to be called uncle no more?" Or words to that affect.

    This led into mother telling the story of Marie being late for school at All Saints, as she had been picking wild flowers on that field. They were for her teacher who scolded her for being late and threw the flowers in the bin!

    Marie would have been living in Legge Street at the time and quite possible with her dad (Benjamin James Owen who had re-married Maud Allen) and the other children barring my mom. Marie was 3 years old when her mother died (Sarah Ann) and George and Jane (Gin) took in my 6 week old mom, and also wanted Marie as well. They were denied the opportunity of doing so by her grandmother as they were newly wed. Mom can recall coming out of the cinema at Dunstall to be met by Marie who broke the news that she was coming to live with them at First Avenue. Mom can remember saying, "What forever?" When Grandad George was asked if Marie could come and live with them, he was supposed to have said that "he wanted her in the first place." At the time Marie was thought of as being mom's cousin – to find out later that she was her sister. This came about a few years later when mom realised she was adopted. Marie passed her 11th Plus and could have gone to a school for higher education. She declined the opportunity to do so, going to Prestwood Road instead. Marie later confessed that she regretted making that decision, stating that she done so because of the financial responsibility that would be put on the family. In later life she became a teacher herself in Harlow.

    I can recall from my childhood going to see Uncle Noah and Aunt Lil Williams when they lived in Devon. I believe that they had purchased a farm and then moved to a Manor House. A story told to me is that a sealed door of a cupboard was found with old fashioned clothes inside.

Marie (Marion)

MOTHER'S WRITING (DOROTHY):
My three elder brothers and sister served in the 2nd World War with the younger ones adding to their ages. The eldest brother (Ben) wasn't very pleased, especially when an officer became suspicious of Eddy aged 14 and questioned him. He had to tell him the truth that having no parents, they were being passed from home to home around the family. The officer agreed to let it stand and not to divulge the real age. That was fine until they found out that the youngest was now on a shilling a day compared to their sixpence!

When my father was alive they lived in Legge Street, Parkfields and somewhere in Chapel Ash after the boys left home. My elder sister came to live with us when she was eleven. It was considered too much by a grandparent and had to go to live with father when he remarried. She passed her 11 plus to go to high school but not wanting to give them the expense of buying a uniform told them she didn't want to go. She told me years later that it was her biggest regret.

We would go to bed not knowing if we'd have to get up and go to the air raid shelter. We could hear mom and a neighbour talking outside with their tin helmets on. We felt safe having mom on guard while dad was at work or on fire service duty.

If the sirens sounded we went to the shelter, except grandad. "If I'm going to die, I'll die in my bed!" I used to worry about him.

When I was 11 in 1940, I was roller skating in the street when I saw a plane. People were shouting that it was German and was dropping bombs. I was so frightened my legs wouldn't move and I was dragging myself along the fence. My elder sister ran past me to get Jan our younger one and dad, with gas masks under his arm picked me up and ran to the shelter and threw me in.

I felt very upset when I found out that I was adopted and for a few years it altered my personality. I think I may have been rummaging around upstairs nearing Christmas and I found some paperwork. I started playing truant from school, and was not very nice to my mother. Silly really as I didn't blame my dad, I was young and it had been a great shock.

My brothers were in the army at the time, stationed abroad and I didn't see them for years. I spent time at other aunts and uncles and one of my aunts told me the facts, that the people I thought were cousins were my brothers and sisters. I don't recall discussing it with anyone else and it must have been consolation knowing that I was part of the family.

I would be aged about 16 when at a brothers wedding reception (Eddy) I was introduced by him as his young sister. This was the first acknowledgement and I felt very gratified.

We had an uncle who had 3 shops, a Grocery and a Fruit Shop in Rooker Avenue and a store in the Scotlands. I worked there when I was about 16 and my aunt was the manageress and I once said "I don't want to be old, I want to die when I'm 40!!! Famous last words. When the war was on mom got a few under the counter perks. From there I went to work at Ever Ready.

Upon leaving school I worked as a waitress, first at Stantons, then the Gaumont Cinema, then at a restaurant in Wolverhampton. It was here when I was called into the staff room to hear announcement on the wireless that the war was over. I had been standing on one side of the kitchen when the owner beckoned me over. He pointed to a pipe above where I had been standing and upon it was an enormous rat! They were common in the town at that time and Health and Safety in 1945 was minimum.

I enlisted in the ATS in June 1948, trained in Guildford then stationed at the Officers Training Centre in Liphook, Surrey (not as an officer). Whilst on one of my leaves I stayed with a friend in Gateshead. One evening we went to the theatre and sat on the front row of the balcony. The manager went on the stage pointed us out to the audience who gave us a standing ovation. How embarrassed were we. Three or four years after the war people in uniform were still very popular.

I was stationed abroad and went out on the troop ship Empress of Australia to Fayid, Egypt. After being there a short while I was involved in an accident. I've had 3 accidents in my life so far, one when I was thirteen and riding a bike with no brakes. I couldn't stop and got caught between two lorries. Another when I was in the army and riding pillion on a motorcycle and the last one (I hope!).

In Egypt when walking with others, an army lorry ran into us and I was the most seriously injured. Whilst in British Military Hospital there, each morning the surgeon would visit and ask "how is my little ray of sunshine? This one morning upon being asked, I became quite upset. This led to my crutches being hurriedly made for me and he said that "he wished some of the men was more like me".

I came back to England on the hospital ship EL. NIL. I was in the company of 3-wounded soldiers who seemed to have been asked to help care for me. People used to say it was like "the blind leading the blind!"

They used to moan when a certain Scottish patient came into join our company as they didn't care for him much. "Here comes that bloke again" they would say.

I spent a few months in the army hospital at Aldershot where I had met Jock and he became my future husband. I was medically discharged from the army and because of my injuries was awarded an army pension.

Jock and myself were married and as he was still in the army we went to live in Blandford. He was stationed at Bovington Army Barracks. We had our first son and then came to live in Wolverhampton after Jock was demobbed.

The first time that Jock met mom and dad was when he came to Wolverhampton on leave. Mom had brought a nice piece of fish for his tea. I was flabbergasted when he said in his Scottish accent "that fish wasnae caught yesterday or the day before, or the day before that!"

I had a few more jobs, another 2 sons along the way, finished my working life as the Manageress of the Canteen at Delta Rods, Bilston Road.

To conclude, what did I know of my real mother? Not very much but I do know that my father loved her and it was a happy home. My elder sister made me imagine that she was ladylike. THE END

ONESELF AND THE SENSE OF MORALITY;

North Castle Street, in St Andrews, Fife holds plenty of my Scottish family history because my Traill ancestors lived there. Their place of dwelling at that particular time is no more. There's a church there now, built in the early 1900's. I've never been inside the church but I have in the small courtyard many times to read names and memorials. Incidentally, the name of the aforementioned church is All Saints; the very reason why it interests me so much. Reason being is that my Wolverhampton family history is to All Saints and area that we know of; often mentioned is that my mother was born within a few yards of the church, which appears to have made a life-long influence. I would be an infant when first entering this church; unmissable - prominently positioned on the corner of Steelhouse Lane and at 5 years of age the biggest building that I had been in. Captured, by a child's eye; 'high, high, high,' timber roof high; where my thoughts were. There's the window that my family could see!

Scottish Wulfrunian
creating writing of RKB ©
since 1989

Oneself and the Sense of Morality

(46) **Oneself and the Sense of Morality** ©

You have something to do with morality All Saints,
the essence of how I behave;
gave guidance, direction, a wall of protection,
when life is difficult, challenging, problematic.
You have something to do with morality All Saints;
off I went on my travels, into the big world,
taking you along; keeping in tune,
with extreme gratefulness in song, learned in infancy;
getting the words wrong sometimes, getting them wrong.
You have something to do with morality All Saints;
yes, a path what they term as right,
thankful for life, keeping honesty in sight.
Captured, by a child's eye;
'high, high, high,' timber roof high,
look at the windows, colourful windows,
stained glass windows;
bright is the daylight,
shining white through the windows,
'bright, bright, bright.'
Morality All Saints;
three score years later, I revisit, research;
cemented, my family history,
in this prominent sandstone church.
Not a shadow of doubt observing
the day by day spectacle,
architectural skill and design;
important, worthwhile in keeping of gothic style,
the additional plans and extensions
that became mine in my childhood.
While musing over morality All Saints;
steadily emerging is a picture of open land
brick works, coal shafts; horse and cattle grazing
and typical British terraced type housing,

nearing closer to town.
Days of past-time, 1877 to 79, construction, consecration,
people, worship and prayer, my family included,
dressed in Sunday best, among the hundreds there.
Captured, nae! invented I say more like, by a writer's eye;
'high, high, high,' thought-they, timber roof high,
look at the windows, colourful windows,
stained glass windows;
bright is the daylight,
shining white through the windows,
'bright, bright, bright.'
My sense of morality All Saints;
acknowledging, pushing forward or following;
direction or manner termed as wrong or right,
thankful for life, keeping honesty in sight;
self-discipline, principles, rules and values:
Credit where due All Saints;
in the making of growing up me,
was a huge contribution by you.

STARS OVER CALVADOS; A good enough reason far beyond any other is to be here at crossroads on Deansfield Road, thinking of stars shining over Calvados in France. I stand to be corrected but every sign in this particular road is fixed to houses. I look up that road and down, thought of wartime and a young man who was 'everyone's friend.' I positioned my poppy from my hat on a lamppost and took a photograph.

This may have been where mom's brother Jim had taken her when she was age 14 to see family. Her aunt sat down and held her heart because she was shocked to see that my mom was so much like Nancy (Sarah Ann); mom's birth-mother. During my research I was to find that it was Deansfield Road; an area I was to become familiar with as I attended Eastfield and Deansfield schools from 1965-69. My mom was 14 in 1943 and 90 when we are having this conversation. It all came about because we had been speaking of family. She mentioned 'Jack,' a pilot who was killed in the war, and that it may have been his parents who Jim and herself had visited.

    In family terms Jack and my mother would be cousins as their dad's, John and Benjamin were brothers. A message from Sylvia, daughter of Ken and Sybil, had been a surprise; Jack's brother lived in Codsall where I live. I was to find his address in the phone book. I know that road well as I walk along there regularly. I did so that afternoon and as I was counting down the house numbers, I noticed a gentleman on a drive putting his car away. I asked him if his name was Owen? He told me that it was and after we had been talking for a good while on his drive he invited me inside. Fred Owen, a widower and retired accountant, had just turned 93 and his birthday cards were still on the mantelpiece. Fred and my mother can't recall ever meeting but they must have because he attended one of uncle Ben's parties; it may have been at the Black Horse. We all would've been there as mom helped with the arrangements. Upon mentioning this she vaguely remembers being introduced to him near the end of the evening, not realising who he was.

    Fred appeared to welcome my company and gave me a great insight of the fatal event of the aeroplane crash. They hit an oak tree full-on and what I didn't know is that there was a survivor. The rear gunner who was an Irishman. A telegram had been sent to Jack's parents and it was a good month or two afterwards that his death was confirmed. Fred showed me photographs of his parents John and Louisa, Jack in uniform plus with other crew members and a plane in the background. There was a deeply touching one taken with his fiancé. It was hard to believe that it was only the day before that I was on Deansfield Road not knowing exactly where the family lived. With regard to the house number, Fred told me which one, coincidentally I had parked my car just around the corner to take photographs.

(47) Stars Over Calvados ©

In Vire, Calvados, France -
four Commonwealth graves
are in line
Flight Sergeant Rock, Sergeants Thornton
and Whalley
and Flight Sergeant Owen,
from the Owen family of mine.
They look clean, very much so light;
I should imagine can be seen at night;
here they lie, four men of the 138 Squadron,
under a Calvados sky.
Flight Sergeant Owen, from the Owen family of mine;
tis time of the year to show our respect;
you went to war to protect
and rid the threat against our shore and ally.
An RAF pilot age twenty one
a son of John and Louisa of Deansfield Road,
from the living world had tragically gone.
Indisputably, intense sorrow of parents and siblings,
at home in Deansfield,
tears and sadness replaced family laughter
for a long long time thereafter.
Officially as John Owen - mentioned in dispatches;
far from your Wolverhampton hometown you be;
you as a person, a description in your inscription,
says it all for me;
'To a beautiful life came a sudden end;

he died as he lived, everyone's friend.'
Flight Sergeant Owen, 'Jack' in the Owen family of mine;
repose en paix, (RIP) as stars over Calvados shine.

Comment from Sylvia; 'Visited these graves in Vire twice. Beautifully kept in a part of the civilian cemetery and well known to the locals we met. The first time we went with my parents, Ken and Sybil was by coincidence 40 years to the day after Jack was shot down.'

The photograph of John 'Jack' Owen was supplied by his brother Fred Owen. He also told me that Ben, Ken and Eddy spent much of their time on leave from the army at his house. Mom hardly saw them at all during the war years. She spent much of her time at Jim and Nell's who lived in a terrace house near Springfield Brewery. Jim served in the Special Police Force during WW2.

WOLVERHAMPTON ROLL OF HONOUR WORLD WAR 2
Owen John Flight Sergeant (pilot) 1166741 138 Sqdn. Royal Air Force Volunteer Reserve John and Louisa Owen, of Wolverhampton. Mentioned in despatches. Died - 26 July, 1942. Aged - 21. Memorial - Vire New Communal Cemetery - Calvados, France. Plot L. Grave 2.

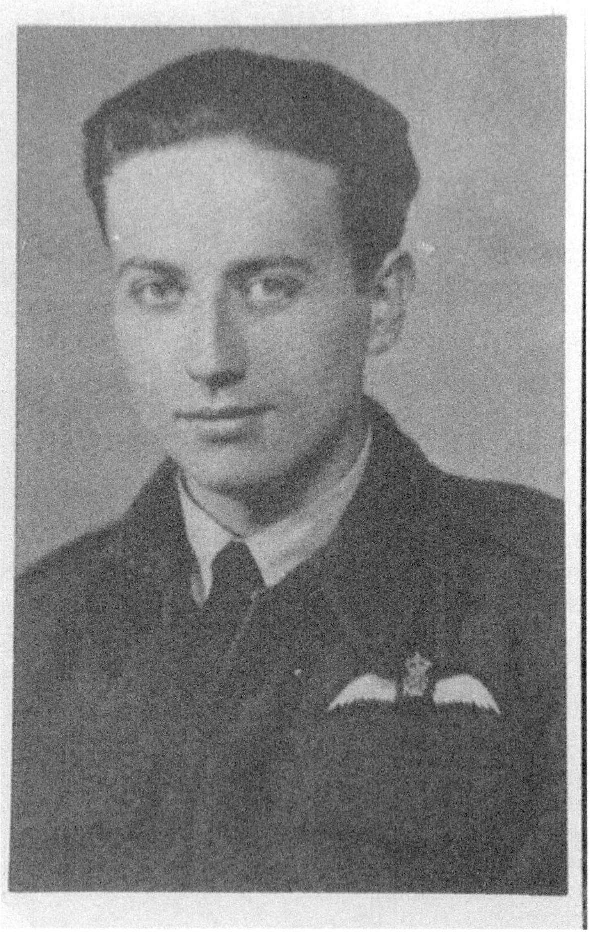

BE YOURSELF; Without nothing to do in particular, I decided to catch the outgoing bus from Codsall to Hordern Grove. I could hear the chiming of church bells as I walked down Crowther Road all the way to Tettenhall Road. In my growing up years when living on Rough Hills the other side of town - mom worked as a waitress in the Newbridge pub. I always thought that it was a fine looking building and seemed further out of town that it is now. I spent a few minutes looking down on the canal at Newbridge; transporting the old mind it did into another world.

In days gone by and before creating a passing through The Rock - the Tettenhall Road turned just past the shops and crossed over the old small canal bridge that I'm looking down on. Grey clouds started to break with an occasional glimpse of blue sky. Part the way up Tettenhall Rock I turned off towards St Michael and All Angels Church. Soon gone has that twelve months since I was in attendance on Remembrance Day. I can also recall my cousin Andrea and Rob Tipton's wedding there.

I browsed about the church yard for a few minutes. While doing so I could hear the organ playing inside on the Sunday morning service. At my last step when leaving into Church Walk - something made me turn around. I did so and saw a wonderful Autumn view. Colours you only notice in paintings and on television.

On to the Codsall Road through Claregate, checking the time at every bus stop. Crossed over the road and down towards Dam Mill. For almost a whole minute it fell silent, all because of no traffic. I was in past-time and wished for a visitors pass to be issued to me as I wanted to be in that moment for longer.

The slight rising of the road up to Birches Bridge raised the body heat; realising I had over dressed, why did I bring that brolly? The return bus that I was going to catch back at Hordern Grove beat me to the bus stop by Bilbrook Station by only a few seconds! A short while later I was back home; two hours of being myself, thinking, imagining.

A Wulfrunian Way

Scottish
Wulfrunian

(48) **Be Yourself** ©
When there's nothing to do in particular
find somewhere to free yourself,
be yourself, you may not even know yourself,
but when you get to know yourself
you may then surprise yourself,
when there's nothing to do in particular
nothing to do but to think of anything else
other than about yourself.

BEYOND THE REFLECTION; This is a follow on from my writing titled 'Be Yourself ' where I had taken in Newbridge during a walk of mine. It was mid-morning when I drove from my home in Codsall and parked in Aldersley - soon to be treading the wet and muddy old railway path back to Newbridge where I was on Sunday. I returned as I wanted to follow the short but interesting old route up to Tettenhall village, once sited in Staffordshire but now Wolverhampton. This was a difficult journey as all travellers had to climb Old Hill until late in the 1820's. The Smestow Valley Local Nature Reserve sign welcomed me just beyond the A41; as always the road was probably busy but peacefulness won over. I viewed the old bridge from different directions and imagined folk of their day coming and going. I am not sure where the beer house was back in the day before the Newbridge pub but nevertheless I searched to no avail for its whereabouts. I looked up towards Cupcake Lane Tea Room as an imaginary train pulled out of the station and away towards Wombourne. For me it is a slight rise in Meadow View, right and left beyond Tettenhall lights and left again into Old Hill. The gradient of Old Hill and the weight of the horse drawn carts and their load must have been challenging for those strong mammals. I listened closely and forced myself to hear the echoes of horses hooves. After a short walk about Tettenhall village it was back down Old Hill. I returned to the old bridge and the important dignitaries were still in deep discussion of how to implement the road alteration and the Act of Union 1801. It was the 19th century - they were so engrossed in conversation that they did not see this man from the future witness their plans when walking down onto the canal towpath towards Aldersley.

A Wulfrunian Way

(49) **Beyond the Reflection** ©

Lost in a world
caught up in another time,
seeing beyond the reflection
in just a little sunshine.
Give me scenes
past-time of kings and queens
show me natures colours
gold, rustic brown and greens.
At the old bridge I stare
important dignitaries are there
curtain opens to a bygone age
I have grand circle viewing
and the old bridge the Grand Theatre stage.
Barges soon to be mooring
on paper, they're pencil drawing;
not long gone had the Act of Union of 1801
all changed, roadway to be rearranged
the London to Holyhead way
plans were in progress
important are the people pointing
and decisive is their say.
They built a new bridge
and blasted the rock
to the road that we know of
that climbs up to the clock
steep is Old Hill, going up, coming down
transporting was described as difficult
to and from Wolverhampton town.
Give me scenes
past-time of kings and queens
show me decisions and reasons
and natures beautiful seasons.

A Wulfrunian Way

They altered the direction
I witnessed their planning of
this London to Holyhead section
when lost in a world
way beyond the reflection
of just a little sunshine.

TH' LADDIE IN TH' CARDIGAN; When you wake in the night and attempt to get yourself back to sleep but your heads not having it. Saturday and what I have to do is already turning over in the old mind. I think of my family, my past, their future; sometimes I just need rest and not sleep. While awake I write and revisit what I have written at a later date. I forget, I surprise myself, I'm impressed and again not. Only yesterday I found work of mine on my phone that I can't recall writing. So I add to it and it springs to mind. I must try again to get to sleep as it's early on a Saturday and almost time to get up!

My thoughts appear to have been focused on a photograph, glued on a home-made calender for the year of 1958; April would be my 4th birthday. I remember that wallpaper so much. It's a picture of Nan with her grandsons of that time. Gareth, looking quite serious, Michael on her lap in that typical baby pose, Piers, then me, in my cardigan. It appears that none of us had yet been told to smile and look at the camera!

A Wulfrunian Way

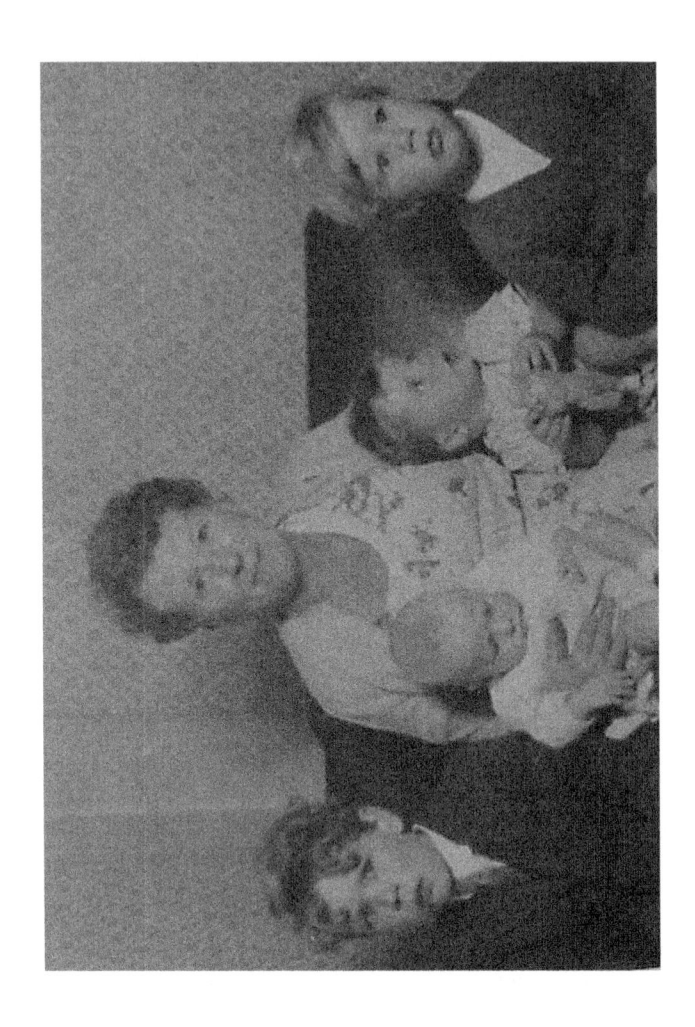

(50) **Th' Laddie in th' Cardigan** ©

Concentrating on something
or it seems, th' laddie he dreams,
heartfelt, butter wouldn't melt,
looking at someone
or it seems, th' laddie he dreams.
No, he's awake, he's alert,
occasionally he'll get hurt
yet to carry a scar
th' laddie in th' cardigan.
Concentrating on someone close
maybe something far,
or it seems, th' laddie he dreams.
He'll kick an' fight,
he'll wake in the night, he'll write,
compete, he'll win and suffer defeat,
he'll be loyal, honest and true,
th' laddie in th' cardigan
at home on the Rough Hills
he'll grow to do things that laddies do.
Look closely, it may seem,
that th' laddie in th' cardigan
he's wondering and pondering
and tonight he will dream.

KING OF BILSTON; Pounding some pavements in Parkfields today at a far less pace that I used to do when marathon training. I walked past the house that we sold over 30 years ago; this Steven's first home. Down to the traffic lights I wandered with memories surfacing in abundance. I turned right, straight on is Bilston where Uncle Ben always told us that he was the 'king,' and there was no reason to doubt him.

A Wulfrunian Way

While on the Birmingham New Road a jogger came running towards me - it could've been me in my imaginative mind, but suddenly there was a 'walking home from work feeling' to the avenue where we lived. It was an upstairs corner maisonette and like ours, it was daughter Marie's first home. I looked up at the kitchen window and imagined myself bottling home brew beer; and Uncle Mick and myself in a photograph with a pint glass. My daughter Marie is in my arms and it looks as if we're using her as a taster! I passed the council garage that was ours, and the bus stop to town on Wolverhampton Road East, that I stood at, then onto work in Monmore Green. This was the days of my 20's and early 30's and I had the feeling that this area had never let me go.

You know that saying of 'only seeing extended family at weddings and funerals.' After saying our sad goodbye to Alan, memories of our Owen family was nice to hear. We were catching up with time and to be quite honest it was nice once again to be introduced to Christine as "Robbie, Aunt Dot and Uncle Jock's son." She seemed really pleased to see me and lots of questions was asked.

Football was never too far away in conversation or trying to remember the name of cousins, a pet horse and a pig! We all at sometime or other in conversation mentioned Uncle Ben; author and soldier of Popski's Private Army. We had a common interest of Wolves & football and I can recall him taking me to away games at Stoke, Rotherham, Arsenal and Chelsea. Apparently he was also 'King Isaiah of Bilston,' as you will read in this book, it was 1957 when he announced the fact that we were related to royalty!

A Wulfrunian Way

Aug 21st 1957.
The Great King Leigh
of Bilston. As you see
his one eye is higher
than the other.

Taken by that famous
foieographer, Robbie
Bennett of "STUDIO
BENNETT"!

(51) **King of Bilston** ©

Fiddly diddly dee up a guzgog tree
so sang uncle Ben,
it was well known in the family when
he served in Popski's Private Army.
He took me to see the Wanderers
home and away games, told me of players
and why they're famous names.
We've got photographs in the family
especially of my brother and me,
fiddly diddly dee up a guzgog tree
taken by uncle Ben.
I study those pictures now
and how they tug at my heart,
in the house, garden and Bridgnorth
never shall those images and I part.
Mom and dad, late twenties and thirty
happy, pulling a face and dirty is me,
fiddly diddly dee up a guzgog tree
thanks to uncle Ben;
the self-claimed King of Bilston
named Isiah, for having one eye higher!
Years have fled
and I sing daft songs as well,
not going to say which ones
as I'm not that silly to tell,
it's when the grandkids come to call
inside of the house or garden,
trampolining or football;
taking photos I do that too
thanks to you-know-who;
Corporal of 'B' Patrol....uncle Ben.
PPA and war time bravery

shall stay forever with me,
fiddly diddly dee up a guzgog tree
good old uncle Ben.

BUILDINGS AND PAST TIMES; I was in need of a few miles on the old feet so I planned a route away from the everyday roads that I mostly walk. Firstly it was a number 5 bus journey to Wolverhampton, taking advantage of my new senior citizen bus pass. I can't believe I'm that age because when the body defences are quiet the mind kicks into gear and suggests that I can do things like I used to. Such as "put on your running shoes and let's go jogging." I wonder if I still can? "He won't get far" says the wakening body "as he's bound to pull a calf-muscle - and what about his dodgy arthritic knees!" Once the debate was over, I accepted the decision that walking is the best option for me. I got off quite lightly as my back problem wasn't mentioned.

Once in Wolverhampton, I stepped out into modern architecture, some older buildings are still on a stage with young actors and actresses, I was there to see the age-old ones in the cast. They were few and far between, as a modern day tram headed towards the junction which was a traffic island by the Horse and Jockey in my younger days.

Monmore Green apparently at one time was a so called 'no go area.' A story I have heard a few times is that a policeman and his bike was thrown into the canal. Thankfully for him he was eventually accepted and allowed to cycle through. Another who I have been told was accepted was Uncle Ben. I can recall knowing that we once had relations living on the Bilston Road near the railway bridges by Monmore Green School. Uncle Ben used to visit those relations with one being 'Stopper' Owen who played for the Wolves. I don't know his first name and yet to find if this is correct or in what team he played. Having mentioned that, there must have been some link with Wolves for it to be known in the family.

I see me, a young man of aged 15, walking through the gates at Delta on Bilston Road in the early years of working life. Before that the canteen where mom was manageress and she had to hurry and dry my football kit as I was playing for the school. The Victoria House pub (War Office) where a Christmas break-up couple of hours was spent. Before that time was the shop where I was a paper-boy. Even earlier days, there is George Dugmore's and my gift of a bicycle. Only about a mile from the bus-depot and I have walked back 60 years. I turn around to see that most of those buildings and definitely that those days have gone. I felt like it didn't look mine no more - as if it ever was? I crossed over the road as it was free of traffic. Suddenly for a few seconds it was silent and felt like the past-time that I was here for.

I carry on towards the road that for a few years was my marathon training route. Most mornings I would run from my home near the Parkfield Tavern, down Dixon Street and towards Bilston. Mentioning pubs, I look over at The New Inn and remember one special night in there. It was the only time that I can recall that dad had a member of his Scottish family visit. Willie Bennet, then living in Toronto stayed with us for a few days.

Through Stowheath lights picking out what's changed and what hasn't? I made a small detour and rang the house-bell of an old work colleague of mine from Narrow Aisle UK named Denis Bailey. The surprise on his face when he realised it was me was lovely to see. Thirty minutes later I was back on track up Wolverhampton Street. At the far end is where my mother-in-law's family lived and her father, Tom Young, was a barber and cut hair in the front living room. When on the Millfields Road it was a strange sight not seeing the club at Springvale. Weekly discos when in my youth and the last time was a humorous evening listening to former Wolves player Steve Kindon.

It was memories in abundance at Ettingshall lights. Beside the public houses demolished, one such time was when I was fully focused on fitness and marathon training. I was cycling and waiting at the lights to turn right from Ettingshall into Parkfield road. A familiar voice and hello from a car driver made me turn my head. It was a former teammate of mine, Terry Bailey who told me that the Woodcross WMC football team had folded. I was staggered as it was a huge part of my sporting life.

I was now on D'uberville Road and once again I surprised a former workmate named Fred Lambert who was about to drive away from his house. He followed my football life very closely did Fred, always watching me play for Sedgley Rovers and Woodcross. A few minutes later I was walking up the road that I was raised in. It's really strange as I instantly recognised two circular drain covers on the footpath. Just as you do a freckle or blemish on someone's skin. Why, I don't know?

The 'new builds' off Steelhouse Lane are appearing quickly and soon there will be new life in the area. An air ambulance helicopter hovers noisily overhead which concerns me. As does the fire-truck a few minutes later that hurries towards and past me. Soon I am negotiating how I can get from one side of Bilston Rd to the other? I eventually arrive back safely at the number 5 Codsall bus stop that takes me home?

A message sent to me from Andy about the above writing was heart warming;
'Dyu know summat Robbie.. next year I'm gonna do this.. I'm going to walk down memory lane, starting in Low Hill and record all my memories for my grandkids.. cheers I feel very inspired '

Cut from a gift made by my mother 26 Sept 1993

(52) **Give Me a Room Back in Time** ©

If you could walk into a room back in time,
where would it be?
I shall not give you one choice,
I'll give three.
My first is my grandparents lounge,
second a particular bar
and third is my wedding
where my bride and family are,
give me a room back in time and a reason
and I shall go far.
Give me feelings,
old fashioned Christmas decorations on ceilings,
give what I'm worth as I ask for the earth,
yes, if it's possible,
give me the impossible.
Give me football pitches,
team spirit and rain,
give me childhood and youth to re-live again.
Give me more than three rooms,
give me four,
and give me who I'm thinking of
when I open the door.

(53) **Definitely Parkfields, Not San Francisco** ©

It must've been a youth club, could've been a disco
definitely in Parkfields and not San Francisco.
There's no interest known from a producer
to make a movie of our romance.
She was Parkfields and Bilston,
me, I was Rough Hills and Scotland.

A Wulfrunian Way

When you take your partner home
to meet your parents, introduce to family,
then years later you take your wife further
and introduce her to Scotland...
it certainly shows togetherness.
Those Tamla Motown days were exciting
the sound and beat
takes me down Nostalgia Street.
A youth club, a disco
definitely Parkfields, not San Francisco.
Those care-free days before driving
walking or bus journeys to everywhere.
I wish there was one that we could get on
that takes us to Nostalgia Street.
The Ship and Rainbow is there,
where we enjoyed ourselves most
laugh, before that, the Red Lion on Parkfield Road.
We married young, our marriage is still strong;
nowadays, if I said I was going to Scotland,
she'd come along.
Nineteen seventy two thereabouts;
all spruced-up at the Black Horse on a Saturday night
children, mortgage to buy our own house
responsibility replaced courtship
'twas nudged into the distant past
or in the collection of bits and bobs
stored away somewhere?
Sam Cooke's voice still sounds amazing,
Raymond Froggatt live, the opportunity couldn't be missed.
We moved house, changed jobs,
grew older and wiser, at least she thinks that one of us did!
It must've been a youth club, could've been a disco
definitely in Parkfields and not San Francisco;
where we did meet..... on Nostalgia Street.

A Wulfrunian Way

On a clear day in Codsall

(54) **Staffordshire Looks Me In The Face** ©

As a boy, Sedgley Beacon, was the first high ground
that made any impression upon me.
During school holiday or warm summer evenings
time up there was appealing;
educational even, examining and working out landmarks
especially connected with my upbringing.
Owens in factories by the industrial canals,
Samuel Williams, a miner on Rough Hills,
days before all of the housing, he could see where I be.
As daylight fades and the evening draws in
you'd think that curtains are closing
but lights all around the midlands turn on
a sparkling field appears as far as the eye can see.
It took that boy a while to want to come down and
return to the ordinariness of everyday living.
Years later, the Lomond Hills in Fife;
it was obvious my action was to scale them
and get to the summit
where I could see the bonnie kingdom.
Look o'er the fields my Kennedy,
Anderson and other ancestors toiled
the lanes they walked and be on these fair hills
that they looked up to,
that was a fantastic feeling folks, simply amazing.
Join me as I go further north to Dundee Law,
what a view, when looking down on the Tay
roof tops, church spires, so high you're the first
to witness sunrise in the east, a breathtaking experience.
The auld days surfaced never wanting to lie still.
That Trail lassie of mine that worked in the jute mills,
Bennet, their machining and carpentry skills;
ships built and then sailed out

A Wulfrunian Way

into the North Sea that I look out on.
There are higher hills and taller mountains
so dangerous that people lose their life
for the sheer excitement of an adventurous challenge.
On a clear day in Codsall,
where most of my present days are spent,
from church grounds, I can see into Shropshire
where the Wrekin has had
a couple of visits from this old scribe.
Half a mile away I'm on the hill, my house side of Oaken;
Staffordshire looks me in the face - tests my old eyes,
a hundred thoughts, but I can't think of one to tell.
"Nae' said I, that boy, fifty five years on,
him on Sedgley Beacon,
what he's done, where he's been,
what he's written and seen....and who he can tell.
Truth is, in a thoughtful genuine way,
he appreciates the reader.

Pictured above is my mom and dad's wedding reception at 107 First Avenue, Low Hill. I can remember that house and the veranda quite clearly with the lovely big garden with rhubarb, Rusty the dog and Grandad Rowley's greenhouse.

Rusty, was a Cocker Spaniel dog and like his breed was lovely to have around the house and in the garden. They are great companions and all us grandkids loved him. He'd lie beside us on the grass for ages as we sat there stroking him. They are a sporting dog with excellent ability in retrieving gamebirds as they are eager to please their owner. They also must have a superb homing instinct. We looked after him once while Nan & Grandad Rowley was on holiday. He went missing and Aunt Jan remembers that he walked home to First Avenue from Rough Hills. "The neighbours contacted Shirl who went and brought him back to your house on the bus. Your mom gave him your dad's dinner!"

Many years later I was learn that Great Grandad Williams built the veranda. He also kept an aviary and bred canaries. I can recall a certificate of his on the wall at our house. He use to work for Gibbons, travelling to different towns. This may have been James Gibbons Ltd, St John's Works as on the 1901 he lived nearby at Stevens Gate, later in Steelhouse Lane. He also came to live with us for a while and with Aunt Mill and Uncle Ern. An amusing story is that during the war while working in Liverpool, a mistake had been made on his identity card, naming him Rowley instead of Williams. Nan (Gin) had altered it only for him to be put in prison while they checked up on him. Nan was to laugh at this when he got back home. "It's not funny our Ginny," he said, "they thought I was a spy!"

AS USUAL SHE HAD THAT LOVELY BRIGHT SMILE; I

went on a walk back into 60years of time this rainy Wednesday morning in December of 2018 in what has been a painful few months for me. I parked my car by the shops at the bottom of First Avenue and walked to Showell Circus and back again. I can remember quite well going in those shops near Park Lane and Guy Avenue with my grandad George Rowley. First Avenue in childhood days was much steeper and far longer than it is now!

I paused at the cross roads Fourth Avenue to cross over the road to take a photograph of where my nan and grandads house was. They knocked it down, along with a few others to build other living accommodation. I was pleased to see that the bus stop is more or less in the same position as it was. Right on cue a bus turned up; my mom and brother Gareth stepped on it as I journeyed back into the 1950's.

Same as the others, there was a front-porch with two doors either side. I counted the houses; 101,103, 105........ 107 was in my mind only!

Five minutes later with thoughts in mind I was up at Showell Circus and ready to walk back down. I passed by where the curved green was and family photographs were taken. There is one such picture with dad in a fashionable trilby and Gareth quite young. An old poem of mine of the Paget Arms and family came to mind

Suddenly from light rain, the heavens opened; and in my imagination, I was at the top of the path of 107; a few steps along was the porch and the front door on the left-hand side. I knocked the door, and my nan opened it; as usual she had that lovely bright smile; I felt loved.

(55) **As Usual She Had That Lovely Bright Smile** ©

I looked at my nan today,
as usual she had that lovely bright smile,
as grandad and I waved goodbye
and went to the Paget Arms,
after a stroll down First Avenue of half a mile.

A Wulfrunian Way

I listened intently as he spoke of his first footballing day,
and the feeling he had when selected to play.
We decide to quench our thirst,
so we entered the bar at the Paget Arms pub,
and we found that two had got there first.
Comfortably at a corner table,
my dad and father-in-law were drinking together,
I could hear them chatting about cars,
horse racing and weather.
My grandad and I joined them,
around that table came aunts and uncles in grandads pub,
they told me my nan was in the kitchen,
she'd gone to make us all some grub.
I looked at grandad and thought, that's strange?
as we've only been gone a short while,
then suddenly I saw her,
and as usual she had that lovely bright smile.
Sharon, my beautiful cousin came with a tray,
she had some food for us all to eat,
they were the tastiest sandwiches ever,
with all fine trimmings and from the best cut of meat.
Then I realised that my nan was looking at me
and as usual she had that lovely bright smile,
suddenly I awoke from a dream and remembered,
they've been gone from my world a long while.
So I close my eyes and there I still see
my nan, she's looking at me,
for a moment she's back in my wayfaring world,
and as usual she has that lovely bright smile,
that lovely, lovely bright smile

DAD'S FIRST VISIT TO WOLVERHAMPTON;

There is an underpass between Wolverhampton High and Low Level Stations. Low Level is now out of use but the underpass was still in use until recently as there is much development taking place. I believe that it will be opened upon completion. My older brother Gareth and I were talking to our Mom, who turned aged 90 this year (2019) who told us of an interesting moment in our family history.

She can recall hurrying down that underpass to meet Dad's arrival at the Low Level Station. As she turned the corner of the arch, dad was walking out of the station, he was on leave from the army and this was his first visit to Wolverhampton. Pictured is Dad (Jock) and Gareth, on First Avenue in 1953.

Not long after that conversation I was n the Station pub near where I live in Codsall. We moved there in 1986, a few months after dad had died. I was alone and in deep thought thinking about him and that latest book of our Scottish ancestry. Suddenly a sign on the wall caught my attention; taking back to a time before I was born.

I don't know the exact facts; Dad had rode his motorcycle a long, long way in sleet, rain or snow! It may have been to Nan and Grandad's on First Avenue to be with Mom. They heard his motorbike outside and waited for him to come in. After a while they went out to see where he was to find him still sitting there frozen to his handlebars.

I have noticed his Record of Leave Granted for 30th December 1950, but that could just be me searching for a reason and he could've been in Blandford, Dorset?

(56) **Here's to the Scotsman Who** ©

Here's to the Scotsman who
seaside towns he drove there to,
each and every destination
held the childhood fascination
to play like children do.
Here's to the Scotsman who
made sure we looked at pools and rocks,
ships and boats, harbours and docks.
Here's to the Scotsman who
the way on a map that he drew,
and here's to the Scotsman who
fathered the men that we grew into

A Wulfrunian Way

(57) Out of Nowhere ©
I dream of catching you up
put my hand on your back
mysteriously real as I can feel
the texture of your black blazer;
surprises you a wee bit
you almost drop your fag!
"Happy St Andrew's Day dad" I'd say
an' away we'd go on down th' road you an' I
then in my half-sleep, an 'out of nowhere' reply
"Happy St Andrew's Day laddie."

THE ALL SAINTS RIVER OF LIFE; I found this piece of writing on a device of mine but no matter when first written or where it is still appropriate to this day. It's a story ode, I can't write any other way, about taking yourself, back in mind to when you were an innocent child in the world of schooling. There in your mind there is a question of how you as that child first entered the classroom has turned out? How you got to where you are, the making of you and the recognition. Reading this writing is that it appears to be a bringing of your past life to where you are in your present day.

    I love churches, the distant and close up view of churches. The approach to a village or town and the magnificent sight of a cathedral. The ruins, like my favourite place on earth, St Andrews. Wherever you live, for me, St Nicholas's in Codsall always draws me to to take a walk to there and just be left alone outside in thought. Ive taken a ridiculous amount of pictures of St Nicks. The one and only St Peter's in Wolverhampton, you can see it for miles and you know then that you're not far from home.

Then there's your first one, is it really the only one? The one that knew you before you even knew yourself? I had a family history to this one that I was to learn of after my years at school.

Oh All Saints
how you did prepare?
this child, to grow,
on the river of life to flow

© Robine Kennedy, Bennett

(58) **The All Saints River of Life** ©

My world today
don't you, All Saints play,
don't you play with my mind?
Oh All Saints,
are you kind, oh All Saints?
I hear voices, I hear children
singing voices, they sound real,
oh All Saints they appeal
because they sound so real.
My world today
I walked ahead,
way ahead and walked away,
oh All Saints
Oh All Saints
I never have told,
that I take you everywhere,
everywhere, oh All Saints
Oh All Saints
how you did prepare?
this child, to grow,
on the river of life to flow
into the vast open ocean to sail
Oh All Saints
in all honesty, I pray, that I did not fail.

WAITING TO SEE QUEEN ELIZABETH; Strange how moments in your life reappear without warning. I had been in The Lych Gate Tavern for a birthday drink with Gareth and Stuart. Afterwards there was a train leaving Wolverhampton, stopping at Codsall that I planned to be on. I walked down Lichfield Street, past the magnificent looking Wolverhampton Art Gallery, designed by architect Julius Chatwin and funded and constructed by local contractor

Philip Horsman, opening in 1884. His generosity was recognised with The Horsman Fountain in St Peter's Gardens.

The connecting roads at Princess Square have interesting history as it is where the first experimental traffic light system in England were installed in 1927. There is a blue plaque commemorating the event. I crossed over the road, looking up towards where the Billy Wright pub is now, suddenly I was transported back to where I had been standing on a bygone day.

We were allowed out of school for the visit of Queen Elizabeth in 1962. We positioned ourselves near Princess Square hopefully getting a good view of Her Majesty. It is amazing to think that in 2015 Queen Elizabeth II became Britain's longest reigning monarch.

(59) **Waiting to See Queen Elizabeth** ©

I see this, I squint at that
I walk through Wolverhampton
on the evening of my 62nd birthday
forgot my spectacles I have
and wearing an old man's hat
I glance over to where
I remember standing there
waiting to see Queen Elizabeth
I stalled, if correctly recalled
the year I believe
was nineteen sixty-two
I'd be around eight
yes about that
not needing spectacles
and obviously not wearing
this old man's hat.
In Princess Street,

A Wulfrunian Way

by the railings,
with my mother,
allowed out of school
yes around eight at the time,
without this old man's hat,
and I wonder,
if Queen Elizabeth,
does she remember that?

A Wulfrunian Way

Remembering Wolverhampton ©
Robbie Kennedy Bennett

(60) Remembering Wolverhampton ©

I shouldn't be but
I feel some kind of sadness,
because somehow
everything is changing;
I accept it but
did we really need
to change so much?
The architecture
that we should've kept,
for tourism
the decision was inept;
square buildings now in view
remembering Wolverhampton
as I do.
I shouldn't be but
I feel some kind of sadness
because somehow
everything is changing.
Let's call a halt
if we're slipping
throw down some salt,
don't slide too far
take some action
for proud Wulfrunians
and visitor attraction.
I shouldn't moan
or should I groan,
Wolverhampton is our home
so keep it tidy, keep it clean,
be the smartest
that we've ever been;
let's hand it over
in a fit state

for our children's children
to appreciate,
where they live
and they're from
even though the past has gone
be it of old, be it new
be it stylish again
and fashionable too
remembering Wolverhampton
as I do.

THE POET IN THE PAPER;

I sent an email in January 2020 to Heather Large at the Express & Star telling her about myself and that I had recently published my 8th book. Her reply was most encouraging and arrangements were made for a photographer to visit me with Heather interviewing me a week later. In the meantime Grace, my niece Karen's 9 year old daughter and granddaughter of my brother Gareth, had been told that I write books. She immediately read Awa' th' Rough Hills an' Awa' and taking it into school to show her teachers. A surprise message to me from Gareth was that two teachers were both going to buy a book. Grace was delighted for this to happen and that the Express & Star had interviewed me and I may be in the local newspaper. An email from Heather Large confirmed that my story was being published Saturday February 29th, this being a leap year. Afterwards I sent Heather a thank you email mentioning that Grace had been waiting patiently for the news. She replied by saying that my great-niece sounds like my biggest fan. One day Grace may read more of my books as they are also her ancestral roots.

HEY, HAVE A GUESS WHAT, I WALKED TO WOODCROSS; Monday 2nd March, a grandson's 5th birthday and quite a sunny day in comparison to the dark wet days recently. The land needs a break from wet weather and the river towns need to recover. I took the opportunity to get in a long walk on the other side of Wolverhampton where much of my young life was spent. It was a bus journey to the ever changing town that only the street and road names I am familiar with. It's marvellous really how certain places or the locality of where they once were bring old friends to mind. Shops I remember are long gone from Pipers Row and Snow Hill as I step further beyond the ring-road on another journey into my past. One hour later I am looking at a 'forgotten how good a view' of the West Midlands from Woodcross.

(61) **Hey, Have a Guess What, I Walked to Woodcross** ©

Pipers Row, Snow Hill to Dudley Road
getting close to addresses that
surfaced in the searching of censuses,
1800's, 1901 thereon,
a japanner, another a blacksmith,
Victorians, Edwardians,
thinking of Wolverhampton therein
and of my long gone working class kin...

A Wulfrunian Way

while I was out walking.
Dancing now into the 1970's and Decimalisation
the Ship and Rainbow, discos and bands,
plus our wedding reception;
visual perception,
making sense of what I see, those days,
so clearly they be...
while I was out walking.
Winding like a river does the Dudley Road
the start of the wanderers eleven and 1877,
Wolves, football and Blakenhall.
Old me, is pleased to see the Old Ash Tree still there,
but Fighting Cocks is in a cloud somewhere
of public houses lost, such a shame,
one day their name may mean nothing...
while I was out walking.
Carefully crossing at the lights
then the blood sport of cock fights,
their aggression, an olden day sporting obsession,
giving geographical location to the crossroads as known,
present day and past-time,
this man on this meandering course alone.
Wearing a thistle for half-ancestry
I walked amongst my Wulfrunian history
away from Wolverhampton.
I married there, we lived just down there,
she went to school there,
and she, my sweetheart, she lived somewhere near,
late 1960's, I saw her in a youth club here...
and we went out walking.
Ettingshall Park Farm, along Dovedale Road,
hasn't changed, seems the same, along here I came
marathon training, pushing myself to the limit
sweating and straining, Alf Tupper attitude,
when put to the test, "be your best boy, be at your best..."

A Wulfrunian Way

in the 1980's running around Wolverhampton.
Before the Horse and Jockey
and Robert Wynd, I take a turn
the fire of football in my belly does burn
resonating tremors of my twenties once more
it becomes a 1970's Sunday, game on,
scoring goals, yes goals I want to score...
while I was out walking.
Hey, have a guess what, I walked to Woodcross!
Great days, never to be seen again
but I revisit them in my dream again
walking out in that team again
representing the Woodcross.
Hey, have a guess what, I hung about Woodcross!
By that club upon the hill
all went quiet, time stood still;
waiting for the old pals to show
I've walked to Woodcross, but they wasn't to know,
so in 2020 back on my travels I'll go.
Hey, have a guess what, I walked to Woodcross!
and then guess what?
Wearing a thistle for half-ancestry
I walked back into my Wulfrunian history
there in Wolverhampton.
Along the A4123, went old thoughtful me again,
Thompson Avenue, towards Snow Hill and Pipers Row,
to the redeveloping station
to catch a bus or Codsall train...
there I finished walking.
Hey, have a guess what, I walked to Woodcross!
and it took years, yes years and years,
aye it took years.

(62) **My Recognisable Wolverhampton** ©

Painted by John Constable
I purchased a print of The Hay Wain
from a shop on Bilston Street,
this is where I meet, in old photographs,
my recognisable Wolverhampton.
Gone, the road is gone; I'm expected to soldier on,
in my Wolverhampton.
Born in the fifties, how about the folk before?
meaning the twenties, thirties and forties,
during the 2nd World War;
the new millennium, the longevity of a centenarian,
hardly recognising, their Wolverhampton.
I feel a stranger with changes, a plenty,
but the old memory bank isn't empty,
old photographs are priceless they really are,
then came the late 20th century
and the ever increasing car.
Before I leave and see you anon,
John Constable completed The Hay Wain in 1821
people, places, time is all the same,
ending up in libraries and galleries,
in books or a picture frame;
just like that shop we all meet, there on Bilston Street,
in old photographs, of my recognisable Wolverhampton.

THE QUEUE TO BLAYDON ROAD BRIDGE;

The threat of Coronavirus was closing in with vast changes to our freedom of life. Youngest brother Stuart was in Cannock Hospital at the time having a full knee replacement. I picked him up afterwards as he was allowed out sooner than expected with his operation being one of the last there for the time being. His follow up procedure at New Cross Hospital resulted in only one appointment only; all others were cancelled. Stuart had been struggling for a while with his knee and I can't help but feel slightly responsible. Along with Gareth he had followed me into marathon running. This one year mom had got some navy blue tee shirts with our names in red printed on the front. A humorous time was when I ran the Harlow Marathon in 1985 and Stuart joined me for the last few miles. Unfortunately he struggled a bit with his leg and instead of him helping me along I had to do so for him. It was great for me to be running in the area that Aunt Marie, Uncle Doug lived and cousin Piers grew up in. For a while all us three Bennett brothers worked together at Narrow Aisle UK in Bilston. Other employees joined us on the running craze that appeared to be worldwide. I have a running log from those days and it is quite visible that I was training hard every day and entering many races. It also adds as a diary and some dates have good and sad memories. One is in 1985 when grandad George Rowley died and another six months later when dad passed away. There's also one or two happier moments such as when daughter Marie rode her bike without stabilisers for the first time!

It's early April 2020, I wrote 'The Queue to Blaydon Road Bridge' history will show that it was in the time of the coronavirus pandemic lock-down (COVID -19). Many people across the world had lost their life. Last night in a rare speech the Queen addressed the nation from Windsor

Castle, at the same time as Boris Johnson, Prime Minister was being admitted to hospital. Strict measures had been put in place, 'stay at home, stay safe, protect the NHS and save lives.' Most people were off work and children were not at school, unless their parents were key-workers, and pubs and shops were shut. Social media was an outlet for many to keep in touch with friends and family.

Three weeks into isolation and I opened my Facebook to see a memory from 2014 from my cousin Mick Duncombe, son of my Aunt Shirl and Uncle Bill. It was good to see and get the mind thinking of family and this book so I sent him the following ; 'Remember this that you copied me into in 2014? You said that it was the Cotts on Rough Hills and mom thought that it may have been the cottages in the dip. Our gg grandfather Samuel Williams was born on Rough Hills in 1841. He was a miner and it makes you think that it was in a dwelling just like that. He married Susannah Smith at St George's in 1859. All the best, stay safe.'

A few weeks later I was to receive a message from Wendy, daughter of my Aunt Mill and Uncle Ern; 'Keep sending your poems on Facebook they are really good. You did post something about some old cottages and I remember them they were at the bottom of 'the track's leading down to Parkfield Road. I remember Phil jumping on the roof they were so low in a dip. Good old days .

I was walking along the lane from Oaken to Strawmore Farm, near Codsall looking over at the trees and thinking that we are not out of the woods yet concerning the coronavirus (COVID -19). I could hear a jogger running behind me and stepped aside the lane. A friendly "good morning" was exchanged between us and the change in the weather. "It's better for running" I called as she started to increase the distance between us. I noticed on the back of her tee shirt she had 'The Trail Marathon(s).' I immediately thought of my Trail ancestors in St Andrews and how much I miss not being there so far this year. My early morning walk to the Eastern Cemetery, Cathedral Ruins and Bishop Walter Trail's castle ruins. I returned to the Staffordshire countryside and made my way to The Oaken Arms junction. A vehicle was yet to be seen until that point as traffic sped by, not as busy as usual I must add. Suddenly a low truck passed me by heading for Wolverhampton with 'Eagle Street' on the back. My thoughts went out to my Owen family who lived there in All Saints and where my mother was born. A van with the name of 'Reid' shot me back up to Scotland, to Dundee to be exact and my ancestor who married in 1831. The back and forth went on as a 'Wulfrun' van approached me. Then someone in a low loader by Wrottesley Golf Club (another Owen connection because of Joe Owen being secretary) sounded their horn at me. I politely waved not knowing who it was? Perhaps it was someone who reads this? I crossed over into Stafford Lane towards Oaken, then the fields to get on back to Monday in my Codsall home.

Another time I was In Wolverhampton for the first time in ages. I was 24th in a queue (Covid 19 restrictions) in Queen Square; thankfully beating the showers. Looking around at the architecture and right by where the Tavern in the Town was. Thoughts of Aunt Barb and Uncle Freddy Lavender came flooding back.

(63) The Queue to Blaydon Road Bridge ©

We arrived and parked-up
on a day quite sunny,
three days from Resurrection Sunday
and folkloric figure Easter Bunny,
following government instruction
two meters apart

A Wulfrunian Way

queueing as told,
well under the bridge
on Blaydon Road.
There was even a loop
at the top of the slope,
we pulled ourselves up
without a tug-rope,
there we joined the queue
for how long we didn't know,
at a guess I would say
30 minutes or so.
Like the Grand National
some refused a high fence,
declining to join
and in their defence,
they may have important things to do
not wanting to add
to the long standing queue.
One bloke on his mobile was not so jolly
he came to a halt,
swore and returned his trolley,
at the height of concern it was amusing
this queuing, the time and refusing.
We witnessed a kind gesture
for an elder lady's sake,
someone went to the door
and to the front she could take,
that lady to cut out the time,
of being under the bridge
and the Blaydon Road climb.
This virus needs experts attention
hard working staff of all types
needs a mention,
thanks to all I should say
who face this day after day.

A Wulfrunian Way

We got to the front and
wishing my wife the very best of luck,
outside Morrisons
I read my Kindle book,
as shoppers came in their load
disappointed faces
that bridge at Blaydon Road,
a long time this tale will be told
when summer has passed
and freezing cold,
I shall glance down
from that bridge
and thoughts I shall get,
that long, long queue,
and how could I forget.
Ellen, our neighbour
said you should write an ode,
about queuing at Morrisons
and Blaydon Road.
Let's fight this and move it on
and appreciate every loved one.
So you good folk out there
the very best of luck,
from the bloke in the car
with his Kindle book.
'Avise la fin' my family, my friend
(Kennedy motto – Consider The End)

A Wulfrunian Way

Wulfruna Street Memories ©
Robbie Kennedy Bennett

WULFRUN STREET MEMORIES; Quite often I pass the birthplace and place of final rest of Sir Charles Thomas Wheeler while out walking in Codsall. One such reminder of Facebook reminded me of times past in Wolverhampton.

(64) **Wulfruna Street Memories** ©
'Wulfruna Street memories
started the night off fine,
this child was safe in mother's hands;
love, care and happiness,
quite simply, a golden time'
'twas late nineteen fifty's and sixty's
on the trolley bus on Tuesday,
Stafford Street we're heading on down
from Princess Square and out of town'

YOU HAVE MY RESPECT SIR; It was a pleasant Thursday evening stroll down Wulfruna Street, Wolverhampton as I made my way to Molineux. I was on my way to an event and had decided to catch the train from Codsall. I live by the station so the nine minute journey was a good choice to make. Year upon year I visit town less often but more on more I admire the architecture of the buildings. I never fail to think of my mother, a proud Wulfrunian who is up town very often.

Wulfruna Street has changed since I was child, we waited here to catch the trolley bus every Tuesday morning to nan and grandad Rowley's. Suddenly I stopped as a picture worth taking had caught my attention. St Peter's brickwork and the Art Gallery are different but together like colours of a team. In the picture there is something noteworthy as I recalled that I had previously taken a photograph in another direction. There is a blue plaque of a certain well known gentleman born in Codsall. He is at rest in St Nicholas Church grounds and most often draws my attention. So once again Sir, I catch a moment, this time in Wolverhampton, a respectable moment.

(65) **You Have My Respect Sir** ©

I often walk by Sir and take a glance
at this peaceful setting I take a chance
and catch the moment, a respectful moment.
In past time I often admired your work
not realising, then finding it was by you,
peaceful is the setting
seconds from a morning countryside view.
You have my respect Sir
the Parish of Codsall you earned it too,
I often walk by Sir actively thinking of you,
you have my respect Sir, my utmost respect.

Sir Charles Thomas Wheeler KCVO CBE PRA was a British sculptor, and the first sculptor to hold the Presidency of the Royal Academy.

Born in Codsall 1892

WITH POPSKI'S PRIVATE ARMY;

Those in my Wolverhampton family will be familiar with Popski's Private Army and Uncle Ben who lived dangerously while serving in this unit. Ben Owen was to write a book titled 'With Popski's Private Army.' Today in April 2020 would be a sad one for Uncle Ben as it was announced that Olga Peniakoff, daughter of Vladimir Peniakoff (Popski) has passed away. On behalf of Uncle Ben I posted sincere condolences.

A few months earlier I had found a Facebook page about the PPA, introduced myself and shared some newspaper cuttings of Uncle Ben, plus a photograph of myself with his signed book that was a gift to me. We also have signed books to my children Marie and Steven. Very soon other members made contact with me. One such person sent me this below;

'I visited your uncle many years ago, to talk to him about PPA and my dad JC who was his comrade. He was such a lovely man, who gave me a signed copy of his book and we exchanged Xmas cards for several years until one year they stopped ?. I was filled with sadness. His card would always be the first one I'd receive without fail. God rest xxx'

A while later this message came my way;

'I have just joined this group. I'm a nephew of Ali Stewart (who died in 1998). He and his wife retired to live in Edinburgh after a postwar life and career in Kenya. They had no children. His MBE insignia was bequeathed to me. I'm piecing together whatever I can find about him: although I saw him occasionally over the years we never had an opportunity to talk about his WW2 experiences, so almost all I know has been gleaned from Ben Owen's book with miscellaneous fragments from elsewhere.'

Life's turned back in time listening to his voice on an Oral History on Imperial War Museum. He took me to Wolves away games as a schoolboy. He drove me to football trials when I was 15 years old at Shrewsbury and Walsall, where Walsall I signed for on my 16th birthday. He was my wedding photographer and much more. We always knew that he was in PPA, Popski's Private Army. He published a book about it and gifted his family with signed copies. Shared from friends of Popski's Private Army Facebook page, knew of it but never listened to Uncle Ben talking. I could hear him telling me about the Wolves players of the 1950's and how good they were. I'm a boy again, life's just turned back in time listening to his voice...

In later years, by bringing the family together, he held a few parties at the Rough Hills Tavern on Rooker Avenue and the Black Horse on Thompson Avenue. Unfortunately both public houses have been demolished.

A Wulfrunian Way

VICTORY FOR THAT HARD DONE GENERATION;

I asked my mother this week if she can recall where she was on VE Day 1945? She will be 91 next month and has always been a proud Wulfrunian. She was aged 15 at the time and told me that she was by St Peter's Church but can't remember who she was with? I reminded her that she was working at Povey's in Victoria Street, Wolverhampton. It was here when she was called into the staff room to hear an announcement on the wireless that the war was over. "Oh yes," she replied, therefore she may have gone from there? Since talking about this with her younger sister Jan, she said that she must have taken her as she remembers being with my mother at St Peter's Church and the cross being lit-up. It was during my mother's time as a young waitress she recalls serving some American soldiers; they asked her if she wanted a tip or some fruit. She chose the fruit to take home to siblings Shirley and Jan, this being the first time that youngest sister Jan had seen a banana. Another time brothers Ken and Eddy Owen were on leave and came in with Sybil and Dot. They playfully left halfpennies on the floor underneath the table. In June 1948, my mother enlisted herself in the ATS, trained in Guildford in Liphook, Surrey.

Later, after posting on Facebook I commented that I have been corrected and told that I misunderstood. The halfpennies were actually on the table, under every cup and saucer! I can imagine the humour of the Owen brothers even in war time.

VE Day
© Marie Simmons

(66) **Victory For That Hard Done Generation** ©

Be strong these tough times, be disciplined;
stay home, be kind, be mindful of tough times,
tough times of the Second World War;
shame that we can't let go and celebrate
as that hard done generation before.
This VE Day 2020 memories of 1945
as told by some who were there;
street parties, images of celebration
from town centres to Trafalgar Square.
We are prevented in doing so this time
shan't be nothing like that national scene,
coronavirus has prevented us gathering
rejoicing for country, King and Queen.
Dunkirk, the Blitz, the Battle of Britain,
Churchill defiant and rallying too;
The Union Flag, the red, white and blue
every child, adult and senior citizen,
express oneself for Victory in Europe
with social measures and self-discipline.

Children of Colley Avenue, Low Hill, at the VE Day street party.

The newspaper photograph above is VE Day 1945 with Christine and Alan Owen (arms folded), children of Jim & Nell on front row.

ONE EARLY MORNING NEAR INVERKEITHING;
Much of the family information has been collected from my mother. It has mostly been in the family home in Cheviot Road on Rough Hills. This being the house where I was born in 1954. In that three-bedroom house is a front and back room, both having a York stone fireplace. I can recall our relation Eddie Eagleton building them. So if not done in telephone calls, the conversations have been taking place in the front living room. Eddie Eagleton was the husband of Josie, daughter of Sidney Allen and Ethel Williams. Barbara who married Fred Lavender was their other daughter. When dad walked into the house, everyone knew about it because of his strong voice and Scottish accent. None more so than a mate of mine named Bernard Griffiths. He admitted to me years later that he was frightened to death when my dad walked in.

With the coronavirus pandemic restrictions of 2020, all of the visits to see mom, including her 91st birthday in June, was spent outside in the back garden where memories are a plenty. She mentioned a couple of painful reminders for me as a toddler. One was when I burnt my arm on the boiler in the back place. An unsafe decision of the position of the council perhaps? The other one was when I fell onto the corner of bricks that dad had made to edge a path. I can recall being taken to the Royal Hospital in a lorry. Mom tells me that it was the pop man. I looked around that garden fondly remembering less-painful times of my childhood. Like when we stood on some sort of platforms, pretending to play guitars like that new Liverpudlian group called The Beatles. Later I was to convert the old kitchen council sink into a small cold water fish pond. I sat there for ages watching those fish swimming about in such a small container. This one day Pat was visiting with children Vicky and Leslie. I was outside with Leslie showing him the fish and he appeared to be fascinated with them. I went inside the house for a few minutes and looked down from the upstairs back bedroom window to see Leslie with a brick in his hands. He was holding it just over the water level waiting to drop on a poor fish!

The coronavirus outbreak continued to cause uncertainty with employment and companies not surviving. When talking about this with mom, as far as she can remember, Courtaulds was the first big company in Wolverhampton to close. She then mentions Every Ready where she worked in her early working life. Beforehand she was working at Uncle Noah's shop. Her cousin Barbara suggested that she came to work at Every Ready with her. She did so recalling that the pay was better. It was when she was working there that she enlisted in the army. In recent years, when waiting in the opticians in Queen Street, looking over at the army recruitment building, she recalls that time in her teenage years. Also another, when granddaughter Karen was doing a project for school and she called in for some information. Two soldiers were there and joking asked if she coming to join up. She put them in their place by telling them that she done so here many years back. What I also noticed was a letter of hers to the Black Country Bugle. It was a request to see a photograph, which they duly obliged, of the troopship 'Empress of Australia.' This is the vessel that mom sailed to Egypt on in 1949. This ship has a fascinating history and shall only write of a few. My research finds that ten years earlier, in 1939, this ship, first of three to have that name, made a momentous journey being first that carried a reigning sovereign and his queen across the Atlantic to the New World, serving as Royal Yacht during the Royal Tour of Canada. At her launch, the ocean liner was SS Tirpitz, later becoming a war prize, built by Vulcan AG shipyard in Stettin, Germany between 1913-19. Renamed Empress of China for a few months only, then renamed again to Empress of Australia in 1921. Her final journey was in 1952 when she sailed from Liverpool for ship-breaking in Inverkeithing, Fife, Scotland. This port, with the iconic Forth Rail Bridge in view, I passed by in 2007 when walking the Fife Coastal Path. If I had known this at the time, I would've stayed a wee bit longer as somehow, it was a link to the meeting of my mom and dad.

(67) **One Early Morn Near Inverkeithing** ©

It hurts that I know so much
and we can't talk about it
speak about it, that's life I suppose
opportunity comes and goes.
I've grown to understand
about our roots in Scotland
it hurts that I've learned so much
and we can't talk about it.
I can't ask, you can't tell
you can't see that I fell,
I fell for land of Scotland.
Signs that you may have caught
me running a marathon
wearing rampant lion shorts
displaying something of Scotland.
The first time, new millennium first time
I wandered almost blindly,
finding our path in Scotland.
O'er twenty years gone that you passed on
again I spent some time in Scotland,
I soon returned as something burned
ay something burned inside for Scotland.
I shan't forget, one early morn near Inverkeithing
doing what suits with my backpack and boots,
planned and prepared, somewhat excitedly scared
after driving all night to Scotland.

A Wulfrunian Way

I stepped forth, I still do
and I wish with all might to tell you,
there's light on the path in Scotland.
Near thirty years gone that you passed on
I continue to spend some time in Scotland,
I keep on returning as something's hot an' burning
ay something's burning inside for Scotland.
Still It hurts that I know so much
ay, I've learned so much
and we can't talk about it
speak about it, a father and son,
that's life I suppose
opportunity comes and goes
ay, it went as far as Scotland

OPENLY HONEST; damn foot problem is dictating how long and far I can go on a walk these days. That's not to mention other complaints that niggle away in this worn old body of mine. "You'll regret it when you're older," I was often told. Most probably when I was in a plaster-cast or having had a stitch-job done at the Royal Hospital. The staff there knew me well. Coincidently I drove by there recently and looked at the former hospital building; painful moments came flooding back. Damn foot problem is....oops, already told you that! So I got to the A41 about a mile from home, deciding that I shouldn't venture any further, keeping to a circular walk. Fields look interesting this time of year and somehow I wish that I was more knowledgable about what crops are in there. "Just take a photograph" said the old bloke inside. So I do. Wherever I go these days I am reminded of my past. What time in life does this actually happen? Probably early thirties for me, because it was all about the future of my young family in those days. Everywhere now are those reminders, they appear instantly or you do what I do, go searching for them.

(68) **Openly Honest** ©

I'm back in the day, a far away day...
Concealing much of a stone wall they were
when nearing the Oaken Arms,
clearing the way for fast flowing traffic
on a road separating Staffordshire farms.
Carefully, I step on that narrow path,
containing a hundred, hundred sharp spikes,
concealing much of a stone wall they were.
Thistle after thistle, is embedded deep in the heart.
knowledgeable of my start in life,
and ne'er forgetting previous generations,
in that land further north where they lived;
Me, I'm proud of the fact and openly honest,
accepted as part of my flesh and blood deal,
that's how this old wanderer out walking does feel.
I'm back in the day, a far away day...
even before I was born!
Concealing much of a stone wall they were,
fighting for existence, growing to be noticed.
Thistle after thistle,
concealing much of a stone wall they were,
concealing much of a stone wall.

From West Park, in to town, or should I say the city, through Queen Square as I wanted to take a picture or two of the Grand Theatre, designed by Charles J. Phipps and Henry Gough and opened in 1894. Memories came flooding back and as always I admired the architecture of some of the buildings. I was too slow to catch the rainbow over the Royal London Buildings in Princess Square; but I did catch sight of Queen Elizabeth in 1962. The late 1970s was difficult days for the Grand Theatre with the closure from 1980-83.

A Wulfrunian Way

(69) A Half-Filled Pocket-Money Tin ©

Often, I like to revisit the world that I grew up in,
if only the shop was still there
where a tanner was plenty,
sucking away at a jubbly
until the triangular container was empty;
creating so much fun and laughter
having orange lips for hours after.
I hadn't yet heard of designer clothes
and never noticed if anyone else wore them;
now and then, we'd do odd jobs, run an errand,
if we were willing, may earn anything
from a threepenny bit to a shilling.
We called neighbours auntie and uncle
as close to us as blood,
families borrowed from each other
keeping friendship good.
The Beano and Dandy was delivered,
taking ages to putting down,
the only thought of the future is when,
pocket money will rise to half-a-crown.
We'd go to Aunt Mill's now and then
on the main road called Thompson Avenue;
the regular visit of Uncle Ben,
football was mostly the conversation
and news of relation after relation.
More aunts and uncles and cousins did come,
it was fun, aye it was fun.
If dad was working we went on the bus,
to see nan and grandad, did the rest of us.
There was sad times, unbelievable sad times,
not when I fell and needed a plaster,
but President Kennedy assassination
and the Aberfan disaster;
anniversaries remind and they should,

shocking images take me back to my childhood.
And an action packed childhood was mine
down the road on the field most of the time.
Dirt was always on my knees,
I believe I was a lad very easy to please,
except that I didn't like peas!
Strange because now I love 'em?
Bath night was Sunday,
early to bed for school on Monday;
in my bedroom was a half-filled pocket-money tin...
Often, I like to revisit the world that I grew up in.

(70) **On This Day of a Previous Century** ©

By Rough Hills Colliery and Catch 'ems Corner
smoke from the Parkfield Furnace I could see
as I walked in a previous century.
Houses of estates hadn't yet been built
on this day in a previous century.
Crossing over field after field
where the Birmingham New Road now ploughs through,
horses graze, I see, on this day in a previous century.
I rest, and refresh, to the best of my ability I draw,
a fantastic view in front of me to Sedgley,
on this day in a previous century.
Up Beacon Hill to the tower I climb and climb - back in time;
looking down, towards Bilston Town,
I can just about pick out St Leonard's,
it was clear, it was brilliant, trust me,
on this day in a previous century.
Iron works and importantly the canal
supplying an hardworking industry,
in a previous century.
Later, at Spring Vale, I search for an inn,
for a glass of ale, to tell my tale,
one sniggers, like an unruly pupil at his tutor,

he mocked 'that I'm from the future.'
Afterwards, Catch 'ems Corner and Rough Hills Colliery,
towards Fighting Cocks, stopping on Goldthorn Hill,
to the best of my ability I draw again, Goldthorn Mill.
From there I see open countryside,
miles of farmland and fields before me,
Graiseley Hall to Merrydale
wondering why names were gave
such as The Dead Lad's Grave?
I see church spires of Wolverhampton;
people will come because of the Industrial Revolution.
They'll come from Shropshire, they'll come from Wales,
that's enough of this poet and one of his tales...
of this day in a previous century.

A GOOD REASON TO PAUSE AT CALEDONIA STREET;

A sign on a building caught my eye, 'The Coach House' in Elm Avenue, Bilston. What history is there I wonder? A few yards from the new turnpike road named Wellington Road built in the early 19th century. I had parked my car and was off for a walk around the town. I've run these roads many times, to and from work, and played a few games for the football club down at Queen Street. I still have the scars to show for it! My first call was to take a photo of St Leonard's Church. Not only does Lynne have family history there but I also have. Great, great grandparents Sampson Darby & Sarah Wheaton married there in 1872. Only yesterday I had posted a fictional poem mention seeing the church from Sedgley Beacon. With that in mind, a visit to Bilston was the plan. Kitted out with walking boots and face mask on, I turned back time, wandering and thinking of something to write, waiting for the spark, as I normally do.

(71) **A Good Reason to Pause, at Caledonia Street** ©

A good reason to pause, at Caledonia Street,
not expecting a finishing applause, no, just because,
the glint in sight of black writing on white.
Aye, the sight of black writing on white
and the name of 'Caledonia.'
Thistles and kin of my bloodline within,
Scottish Independence and Wars,
nae bother in Bilston does it cause...
just a good enough reason to pause.

WOLVERHAMPTON THE PACESETTERS
985
1985
1000 YEARS – MILLENNIUM

(72) **A Violin Plays** ©

My town and memories
the land form and setting
shapes of roads and travelling
there to getting but not forgetting,
my town, the old fashioned old town.
The roads to town are different now
some have completely gone,
you remember some and forget
many of them as the years roll on.
Development and the ring road decimated
the entry to the old town
my town, the old fashioned old town.
Twice it came to mind recently
at red lights, what once was
Cleveland Road and Bilston Street,
oh how I wish I could meet young me again
without a care in the world
walking out of Steelhouse Lane
going up town, the old fashioned old town.
The lights turned green
I drove by where once there had been
a road traffic island and the Horse and Jockey
at the start of the Bilston Road
The cooling tower stood prominent
and dominated the skyline,
this part of town
the old fashioned old town of mine
Got a load of memories
of growing up days that plays my mind,
I search and find, can't leave those years behind
so I write them down
about my town, the old fashioned old town.

A Wulfrunian Way

A violin plays reminding me of days
around town, the old fashioned old town,
a violin plays, a singer doesn't sing
lights turn red on the ring road
The spire of St George's I admire
sad it's got lost somehow,
once standing supreme
by where once it had been
serving its purpose for the folk of the old town
A church steeple places and people
let the violin play while I remember the day
of my town, the old fashioned old town
let the violin play

AT THE VERY LEAST THERE'S A ROAD SIGN; This came to mind from posts on social media by Alan Alcock. He had uploaded photographs of the junction of Lower Walsall Street and Lower Horsley Fields at the start of the Willenhall Road. One of those photographs was of St Matthew's Church built in 1849 and demolished in the 1960's. I must add that I did not know this area very well until I started at Eastfield Secondary Modern School. Walkabouts at lunchtime included visiting shops around here. The closest family connection that I can find are my Williams, Darby and Farnell families in Duke Street, York Street and Union Street respectively near Commercial Road in the mid to late 1800's but nothing at St Matthew's. Many comments about the church concerning christenings and marriages was made on Alan's posts, proving how well the church and stores served the community. As I often do, I thought of how this, and other areas of Wolverhampton has changed in my time. My mind's eye is not willing to rest.

(73) **At The Very Least There's a Road Sign** ©

Could be the buildings?
could be the setting, but,
too nostalgic, am I getting?
an area disappeared, destroyed,
saddened more than annoyed,
at least there's a road sign, a street,
but where's the buildings?
It's like they've wiped away my past.
Things don't last forever,
but wherever I go these days
I see changes,
and I can't get used to the changes.
No plans of a complaining letter,
pure sentiment and visual,
most changes, are they for the better?
Hark at me! not considering condition,
my poetic, realistic, important omission.
My mind's eye is not willing to rest,
traffic light changes,
but which way is best?
Wolverhampton that I grew up in,
I preferred, before the changes,
and it's hard to except the changes.
Gradually, they're wiping away my past...
at the very least there's a road sign.

Additional information; Paul Webber, a former football team mate of mine commented on social media that St Matthew's Church was built by his ancestors John Cockerill and Sons of Darlington Street.

Another message came from Paul Bennett, a former All Saints Junior School classmate. "You do have a way with words Robbie, always finding the right ones especially for those of us who who know these streets. In 1898 my Nan, Alice Cockin, was born in Swan St just opposite those traffic lights. The sign is still there. Her siblings and her were baptised in the church. It's in black and white in the church records so we can see them but the building has gone, wiped from sight to all that go by, but still lives clearly in our minds."

THE BLUE BRICK VIADUCT AT DUNSTALL;

Speaking to a couple of bargemen this Friday, October morning. "That's the life" I said to the first, "Absolutely," he replied. When another told me where he is going - I asked him how long will it take? Before he could answer I said, "I suppose it doesn't really matter." We found that amusing. Both of them seemed calm and contented in a way that only being by a stretch of water can make you. For me though, it was more of a physical challenge, as I was on my walk along the canal towpath from New Cross Hospital, Wolverhampton towards Bilbrook. From there it was roadside to my Codsall home. In total it took me almost 3 hours as I am not fast on my feet these days. I had partly prepared a poem about the Dunstall Viaduct and wanted to take an up-to-date photograph of the Victorian structure. Later I received a message from Peter Williams that brought reality to my writing;

'My Great Grandfather moved from Wales to help with the construction of this viaduct in the 1800's. With the money he made he bought the Northumberland Arms Pub on the Stafford Road not far from the viaduct.'

Later, I asked Peter if I could add this information and he replied; 'Certainly Robbie. My great Grandfather was Samuel Evans, came to Wolverhampton from Flintshire. He was a teetotal and at the time, he owned the Northumberland Arms which was at the side of the Great Western Railway bridge, a small hotel used by a lot of racegoers getting off at Dunstall Park railway station. Hope this helps.'

Canals, bridges, their history and people – always interesting to this poet.

(74) The Blue Brick Viaduct at Dunstall ©
Can you recall lad?
when first you saw the Dunstall Viaduct.
On a coach you were
not yet considering a profession
travelling from Eastfield school
for your weekly games lesson.

A Wulfrunian Way

<pre>
      Underneath, aye the coach drove underneath
            you looked at the sight o' the height
             and lucky you were to see I'm sure
            when you watched a train going o'er.
                    Can you recall lad?
              or am I testing your thoughts too much,
                   have you lost your touch
              in bringing on back the old days,
                   the good old, old days.
                    Can you recall lad?
                    fascinated let's say,
         that men could construct such a design
       back in their day, really clever weren't they?
    The roundness, every brick in the viaduct curve,
             they deserve this praise they deserve,
   those admirable Victorian men, for the time when,
             every hand that positioned them,
          those blue bricks in the Dunstall Viaduct.
                  Enjoy your breakfast lad,
          your Braeburn apple that's in your bag.
             Rest a while by number 16 Lock
        as you've walked all the way from New Cross,
      soon you'll be dragging yourself through Bilbrook,
            further away from the blue brick viaduct.
          Shan't ask no more lad what you recall,
                  'cause I bet you'll be weary
       less talkative and cheery lad, tired and weary.
</pre>

STAR OF THE VILLAGE PETE DOODY; I've known a particular Doody family for years, starting when our Gareth was a paperboy when they were on Bilston Street. Mr Doody always appeared to be working out of the back of the shop. I'd hang around while Gareth was getting the paper-sack ready. Mr Doody only had one arm; I didn't know the circumstances until my brother-in-law Terry Baker, who is related to them, told me that is was a works accident involving a crane. Just writing of this makes me visualise former time on Steelhouse Lane that Morris Baker, another relation of theirs, would speak to me about. The houses, shops, All Saints Schools and St Joseph's on Adelaide Street. Morris is a former Football League referee, now a Wolves Academy Scout, who at the time of my retirement reported to me as Head of Local Recruitment.

Assisting Gareth on his paper round in the 1960's made me familiar with the street names near Horsley Fields, Lower Walsall Street and surrounding area. Many years later I discovered some of those street and road names in the birth, marriage and censuses of my family. Duke Street (Williams), York Street (Darby), Commercial Road (Owen), Union Street (Farnell); little did I know at the time how much that they would mean to me in later life.

Before being on Bilston Street, the Doody paper shop was over on Steelhouse Lane, next to the Why Knot pub (I also see this as Why Not?). Over the years I got to know well some descendants of this Doody family. The late Peter Doody snr, Tony a plasterer who I knew first, Dave who lives in Perth, Western Australia, Janet in Glasgow and younger Pete who still lives here in Codsall. During COVID 19, Pete took it on himself to assist in the cleaning up of Codsall village. I started to take a few photographs, posted on social media and wrote a poem about him. This grew a lot of attention and soon plenty of compliments came Pete's way. I even went as far as sending an email to our local MP, although I can't confirm that this assisted in what happened later. I was absolutely delighted for Peter Doody on his Codsall Parish Community Volunteer Award. What's more, he called me the week before, inviting me to be there to see him receive it. For a moment or two, I imagined how proud his parents would have been if they were here - and those Doody forebears of his in the paper shop on Bilston Street.

(75) **Star of the Village Pete Doody** ©

He had some time on his hands
and to himself he wanted to please,
so he got together a tool or two
and got down on his hands and knees.
He filled bags with overgrown weeds
and in time he did succeed,
in making the village a tidier place
did fluorescent jacket Pete,
in his hat and glasses and smiling face.
Now the villagers did appreciate
for The Square in Codsall is looking great,
scraping curbs and parking bays
Pete stuck into most days.
Early morning and late afternoon
outside shops, pubs, businesses and hair saloon.
Now Pete's got himself known
still he gets out there on his own,
deserving a 'pat on the back'
but social distancing has prevented that.
So Peter Doody, you're a star!
wherever in the village you are?
from the chippy to Compton Care,
Blunts to Lloyds Chemist,
not a missed weed anywhere.
Star of the village Peter Doody,
you'll never be shy, big-headed or moody,
keep that cheery smile on your face
helping the village look a better place.

EDWARD OWEN; In my poem, 'A Wulfrunian Way' I mention family names being in Wolverhampton for generations. It was 2015 when Richard Fardoe, son of Sheila and grandson of Ken Owen, found a sad story reported in the Wolverhampton Chronicle in August 1853;

'An inquest was held in the Summer House on Steelhouse Lane concerning the death of 8 year old Edward Owen who had fallen down an unprotected coal pit at Frost's coalfield, Monmore Green. This being only a yard and a half from the road used by people living near. He was found by his father Benjamin Owen and neighbour Joseph Williams.'

Coincidently, both these men named are in my family line as great, great, great grandparents. The family link came 3 generations later in 1915 with the marriage of another Benjamin Owen and Sarah Ann Williams, my mother's birth parents.

ONLY A STONE'S THROW AWAY IS A CHURCH; The family address was Eagle Street, I'm not certain but windows could have looked out on Steelhouse Lane. Across the road is All Saints Church which would have been a fascinating sight to an imaginative child. The view of this Gothic style church, over 50 feet high with a most interesting arch shaped window in the east end would surely attract the eye.

Nancy could look out of a window, if there was one, or stand opposite to see where she married Benjamin James Owen in 1915. Also her parents Joseph Williams and Sarah Ann Darby in 1893. She would be able to see the corner that three decades later I was to turn as a pupil of All Saints Junior and Infant School from years 1959-1964. She may have seen me walking quietly in line into church for the harvest festival thanksgiving celebration. If not me, she probably would have seen children of her own. Sadly the dwelling is no more, therefore my imaginative mind has to take control. I presume that we had family members in the congregation for the Sunday morning services. In the 1920's this was a tight knit area with the schools, terraced houses, shops and public houses. After a hard day in nearby factories or employment elsewhere, would the Owen, Williams, Darby and Rowley men quench their thirst in the Summerhouse, Why Knot, Steelhouse Tavern, Hen and Chickens or any other not mentioned?

The short walk to Wolverhampton town centre was very different that it is today. I wonder if my family spent much time up there, possibly in the audience at the Grand Theatre - watching a show or admiring the architecture of Charles J. Phipps? I certainly look for the faces of my related Wulfrunians on the crowded streets in old photographs. Where were leisurely Sunday afternoons enjoyed in summer. Possibly West Park, or was it East Park as it was closer? I truly hope that the home of the Owen family in the court on Eagle Street had its share of happiness, as there was sad days ahead. Nancy, real name Sarah Ann Owen nee Williams, two days before her 33rd birthday and her mother, Sarah Ann Williams nee Darby, two years later.

I asked my mom the question of what did she know about her birth-mother? Her answer was "nothing really, I can imagine her as lady like kind of person, perhaps because of Marie (Marion)."

A Wulfrunian Way

(76) **Only a Stone's Throw Away is a Church** ©

My drive home is along Steelhouse Lane,
past Eagle Street,
simply because, my mother was born there...
I choose that route as it suits, puts me in a gear,
making former-times appear,
as I have that eye, when going on by.
It's not as it was in the 1920s
a few men talking on the corner
kids playing safely in the road - I say safely,
for a lot less traffic in those days
every child plays outside in those days
It's not as it was in the 1920s
I see it in colour not black and white,
first modern period clues, tight street views,
picking up news from the street corner.
Nancy, I see her calling her children,
I look into her eye, going by...
can't help but give a deep sigh.
Nancy married in 1915
only a stone's throw away is the church.
Nancy, I see her waving to her husband,
her voice I hear, she sounded sweet, so sincere,
only a stone's throw away is a church, is it Sunday?
It's not as it was in the 1920s
I have the ability of making it seem,
I have the sight of seeing it in colour
not black and white.

A Wulfrunian Way

Nancy, my mother's mother,
she's looking me in the eye,
is she wondering, who is that lad going on by?
My drive home is along Steelhouse Lane,
past Eagle Street,
simply because, my mother was born there...
and only a stone's throw away is a church.
Is it Sunday? It feels like a Sunday.

Sarah Ann Owen nee Williams (Nancy)
1896-1929

A TREE PLANTED IN HEAVEN; At the time of writing (2020) 151 new houses are being built on the 8.4 acre brownfield site off Steelhouse Lane calling it Saints Quarter. That means new families and future in an area that holds much of my past. The church and school buildings are not used the same as they were in my day. They still stand though creating many thoughts for me. In that process of thinking are Joseph and Sarah Ann Williams nee Darby; Sarah Ann, who I know her now more as Nancy. Her siblings Ethel, Nell and Jane (Gin), Nancy and Benjamin James Owen and their children - Ben, Jim, Ken, Eddy, Marie and Dorothy, my mother.

To close this book of my ancestral roots in Wolverhampton, must come from another poet in the family, and that is my Uncle Ben, Nancy's first born child. "I think that this is his best one," said my mother. A story poem, which tells of a sad time in the family.

A TREE PLANTED IN HEAVEN

Far away in the distant past
A life I lived which did not last...
Twelve short years it did endure,
So peaceful, happy and secure.....
And then the Queen amongst us died,
But years did pass before I cried.....
And by then the King had gone,
The King the Queen had doted on.....
So six was left to find their ways
Amongst the pitfalls of of the days.....
By great fortune, and the Grace of God..
The six through life their way did trod,
Until one day the second born
Saw the light of his last morn...
But still we six are we
The fruit of such a happy Tree,
From heaven it came, back there it went,
Perhaps once more happy and content....?

Ben Owen

Mom & Dad's Wedding

PROUD WULFRUNIAN; When speaking about my mother to those who don't know her, I always describe her as a proud Wulfrunian. Up until the coronavirus lockdown rules of 2020, she caught the bus regularly from Rough Hills to Wolverhampton. In the new millennium alone she was meeting relations Barb, Audrey, Pat, Shirley and Sheila, just to name a few in the family.

This one day when I was up there early myself, I bumped into her when I was walking down Lichfield Street towards Princess Square. She didn't notice me at first as she had her eyes on something over the other side of the road by Lichfield Passage. I recall that small street quite well from when we used to walk down there to Wulfrun Street, to catch the trolley bus on our Tuesday visit to see Nan and Grandad at First Avenue. As a child Lichfield Passage for me should be included as a scene in a Charles Dickens novel. That's how I imagined the time to be when he was creating those well known fictional characters. It was somewhere near The Posada pub that my mother turned to look forward and see me. She told me that she was looking over at the corner shop where a jewellers used to be. It was where they brought her wedding ring from. Mom and Dad's plans was not to pay a lot but ended up spending a lot more. The ring cost £15 which was really expensive at the time. The jeweller must have been happy as he also gave her a bracelet as a gift.

I was on Stafford Street one day, waiting patiently for traffic to pass by, to take a photograph of the register office where they married. It was easy to visualise them outside on the steps, with Nan and Grandad Rowley, Great Grandad Williams and Aunts Marie, Shirl and Jan. Family, all those pictured and more that give me so much to be proud of.

With the industrial heritage of Wolverhampton - the digging in the mines and grafting in factories; when it came to war, patriotic for their country and protective of family, our ancestors were there, contributing, doing their bit - our way, 'A Wulfrunian Way.'

THANK YOU FOR READING

More Books by the Author

Awa' th' Rough Hills an' Awa';
I consider my poetic writing to be short story odes amongst a bigger picture of life. It is not chapter to chapter writing but story and reason to the rhyme. Childhood memories of the area that had an input into my growing-up years leading into youthful days, courtship, married life and parenthood. This book will take the reader on a poetic journey to the days when the fields near to the Monkey House and Rough Hills Tavern had youngsters playing and the pubs were a hub of activity. All in the life of boy to man, who was raised on the Rough Hills Estate of Wolverhampton. In recent years my writing has reached my ancestral Scotland with becoming a featured poet.

Wulfrunian Footprints in Fife;
My first poetic ancestral journey from my Wulfrunian upbringing to The Kingdom of Fife in Scotland. Inspired by the land of my late dad, a Fifer who met my mother in Aldershot Military Hospital in the late 1940's, married and settled in Wolverhampton. Fife was to become part of my life, walking the Fife Coastal Path and climbing the Lomond Hills, whilst searching my Scottish family roots. From the inland villages of Collessie and Ladybank, to coastal towns of Kirkcaldy and St Andrews then over the Tay to Dundee, another ancestral home. Being where my dad and his forefathers may have worked and lived gave a great inspiration to the writing of this book. All this and more in

picture, story and ode by this man of thought and sometimes thoughtless Wulfrunian.

'Ode' Gold Wolves;

An illustrated collection of my poems (expanded in 2017) related to Wolverhampton Wanderers Football Club, well known as Wolves. Having been born in Wolverhampton of English and Scottish parentage, I grew up to have Wolves at heart. Within a week of my arrival on this earth in 1954, Wolves were crowned First Division Champions. I was raised on the Rough Hills Estate area of Wolverhampton and could hear the roar of the Molineux crowd whenever a goal was scored. It never ceases to amaze me as to where next I shall find a supporter of Wolves.

Kicking around Codsall;

My descriptive poetic writing from our time as a family living in Codsall, Staffordshire, north west of Wolverhampton since 1986. There has been endless dog walks and training runs for me over the fields and down lanes that surround what we call the village. I soon felt part of the community of Codsall due to actively taking part in the games of football on the village hall playing field. Having being a writer of poems and odes for over a quarter of a century, it was time to see if I had enough work to produce a book with a Codsall theme. People, places, sunrises and life events are a few reasons as to why my verses are created.

Jock I've Been to Hampden;

I can still recall the overwhelming feeling when first experiencing the atmosphere of a crowded Hampden Park and the ancestral pride in being there. Scotland and football has always been of interest because of my parentage. The first time at Hampden I recall looking at the Scottish flags flying over the opposite stand and at the rooftops of the buildings of Glasgow. I was there for Bennet's of Fife and

Dundee, Traill of St Andrews and Kennedy of Kirkcaldy and more. Odes related to Scottish football, professional, grass roots or whatever. All because I have an ancestral interest. To experience Scottish Cup Finals and Internationals and wishing that I had played in Scotland myself when a young man. From day one Scottish footballers have always been of interest to me. It must be in the blood.

On a Wolverhampton Journey;

Memories in description, picture and ode of growing up and living in Wolverhampton. Many of the roads I have run in my days of training for the marathon and travelled on to my places of employment. My growing up and then youthful courting years to marriage, parenthood and home loving life. An active sporting man who turned out to be a very thoughtful person by writing many story poems which the Black Country Bugle were first to print. On a Wolverhampton Journey is a local poetic insight into my travel through the stages of my life to the present day. The decision to go ahead with this book was because of Awa' th' Rough Hills an' Away. This being my first book appears to be of local interest. From there my Wulfrunian Footprints in Fife was featured in a Scottish newspaper. 'Ode' Gold Wolves, our local football club where former times and players are remembered. Kicking around Codsall was my contribution to the village where I now live. I have often said that I was not a great scholar in the classroom, therefore to get close to having work published in my name was a fantastic feeling. I have always had an imaginative mind and can easily drift away into thought. People, places and memories inspired this wanderer to write more work to publish this book of Wolverhampton, my hometown.

Back an' Forth tae Fife;

My second book about my poetic ancestral journey from my Wulfrunian upbringing to the Kingdom of Fife in Scotland.

A Wulfrunian Way

Drawn down the path of my dad and our bloodline to villages such as Collessie and Ladybank and to the coastal towns of Kirkcaldy and St Andrews. This is a continuous story that developed after the passing of my late dad. Delving into my roots brought a fascination of life and events in their time that I creatively write about. 'Wulfrunian Footprints in Fife' set the ball rolling and continues with this book 'Back an' Forth tae Fife.' In 2014 came 25 years of writing in which over a decade of that had included a Scottish theme. This being as I was influenced greatly by this historic county of Scotland. The characteristic of the coast and landscape brought inspiration to many of the writings. As I have grown older my appreciation of Fife is a proud ancestral inheritance. The odes within are heartfelt and warming that will take you back to a past that included my Fife ancestors. My imaginative mind created poems of the time of my forefathers in the land of theirs that they lived. New generations have now made this journey back to their roots ensuring that our Fife connection will continue in mind and spirit.

Th' Callin' o' Fife;

In the same theme as my two previous Fife writing but with the added knowledge that I have since first writing my story. One great piece of ancestral interest is the poem of mine and story that brought a 100 year anniversary in Kirkcaldy. Our Trail to Scotland;

A continuous journey of going back to my ancestral Scotland, to those in the bloodline and more who accompany us. The inspiration of the land of our forefathers fires my imagination. This being the fourth book of our Scottish roots written in my creative poetic style. The joy of crossing the border has now been experienced by our grandchildren. Unbelievably family of the next generations have returned to Ladybank. The wonderful sunrises that I speak about in St Andrews have been witnessed, also that view from the Kinkell Braes. The finding of the final resting places in Fife, Angus and Perthshire encourages me to understand who we are. Never in my wildest dreams could these events be forecasted, such as being at the summit of Dundee Law, the volume of writing predicted and ancestors found. Our Trail to Scotland, the poetic journey, those miles from home to home is definitely worth travelling.

EDDIE;

This is a short story based on my poem, 'A Fighting Desire,' that I wrote in 1991. A person's bravery effects everyone that cares for them. Some people handle that worry better than others do. 'Eddie' was first featured in two parts in the Black Country Bugle in 2004 with some name alterations and additional content added in 2020 for this edition. Available in e-book only.

Our Trail to Scotland;

A continuous journey of going back to my ancestral Scotland, to those in the bloodline and more who accompany us. The inspiration of the land of our forefathers fires my imagination. This being the fourth book of our Scottish roots written in my creative poetic style. The joy of crossing the border has now been experienced by our grandchildren. Unbelievably family of the next generations have returned to Ladybank. The wonderful sunrises that I speak about in St Andrews have been witnessed, also that view from the Kinkell Braes. The finding of the final resting places in Fife, Angus and Perthshire encourages me to understand who we are. Never in my wildest dreams could these events be forecasted, such as being at the summit of Dundee Law, the volume of writing predicted and ancestors found. Our Trail to Scotland, the poetic journey, those miles from home to home is definitely worth travelling.

A Wulfrunian Way

All Saints Junior School 1963-4
author seated far right on front row

SCOTTISH WULFRUNIAN
Poetic Writing of
Robbie Kennedy Bennett
Amazon have an Author page
that you may wish to visit
or my website of the above name.

Scottish Wulfrunian
Robbie Kennedy Bennett
rkb2poetry.weebly.com
robbiekb@hotmail.co.uk

Printed in Great Britain
by Amazon